● PERGAMON INTERNATIONAL LIBRARY
of Science, Technology, Engineering and Social Studies

*The 1000-volume original paperback library in aid of education,
industrial training and the enjoyment of leisure*

Publisher: Robert Maxwell, M.C.

GESTALT THERAPY
(PGPS-92)

D0841626

THE PERGAMON TEXTBOOK
INSPECTION COPY SERVICE

An inspection copy of any book published in the Pergamon International Library
will gladly be sent to academic staff without obligation for their consideration for
course adoption or recommendation. Copies may be retained for a period of 60 days
from receipt and returned if not suitable. When a particular title is adopted or
recommended for adoption for class use and the recommendation results in a sale
of 12 or more copies the inspection copy may be retained with our compliments.
The Publishers will be pleased to receive suggestions for revised editions and new
titles to be published in this important international Library.

Pergamon Titles of Related Interest

Kanfer/Goldstein Helping People Change: A Textbook of Methods, 2nd Edition

Lerner Poetry in the Therapeutic Experience

Marsella/Pedersen Cross-Cultural Counseling and Psychotherapy: Foundations Evaluation, and Cultural Considerations

Sarbin/Mancuso Schizophrenia — Medical Diagnosis or Moral Verdict?

Wandersman/Poppen/Ricks Humanism and Behaviorism: Dialogue and Growth

Related Journals*

Analysis and Intervention in Developmental Disabilities
Applied Research in Mental Retardation
Journal of Psychiatric Treatment and Evaluation
Personality and Individual Differences

*Free specimen copies available upon request.

An Introduction

Vernon Van De Riet
University of Florida

Margaret P. Korb
Santa Fe Community College

John Jeffrey Gorrell
Southeastern Louisiana University

Pergamon Press
New York • Oxford • Toronto • Sydney • Paris • Frankfurt

Pergamon Press Offices:

U.S.A.	Pergamon Press Inc., Maxwell House, Fairview Park, Elmsford, New York 10523, U.S.A.
U.K.	Pergamon Press Ltd., Headington Hill Hall, Oxford OX3 OBW, England
CANADA	Pergamon of Canada, Ltd., Suite 104, 150 Consumers Road, Willowdale, Ontario M2J 1P9, Canada
AUSTRALIA	Pergamon Press (Aust.) Pty. Ltd., P.O. Box 544, Potts Point, NSW 2011, Australia
FRANCE	Pergamon Press SARL, 24 rue des Ecoles, 75240 Paris, Cedex 05, France
FEDERAL REPUBLIC OF GERMANY	Pergamon Press GmbH, Hammerweg 6, Postfach 1305, 6242 Kronberg/Taunus, Federal Republic of Germany

Library of Congress Cataloging in Publication Data
Van De Riet, Vernon, 1935 —
    Gestalt therapy, an introduction.
    (Pergamon general psychology series; v. 92)
    Bibliography: p.
    Includes index.
    1. Gestalt therapy. I. Korb, Margaret P.,
1920 — joint author. II. Gorrell, John Jeffrey,
1945 — joint author. III. Title. [DNLM:
1. Psychological theory. 2. Psychotherapy. WM420
V234g]
RC489.G4V36   1980   616.89′143   80-11457
ISBN 0-08-025587-6
ISBN 0-08-025586-8 (pbk.)

Printed in the United States of America

Table of Contents

67541

Acknowledgments

We gratefully acknowledge the following publishers for permission to reprint selections from the works listed:

Random House, Inc./Alfred A. Knopf, Inc., New York, *Ego, Hunger and Aggression* by F. S. Perls, copyright 1969, and *Nature, Man and Woman* by Alan W. Watts, copyright 1958.

Science and Behavior Books, Palo Alto, California, *Gestalt Approach and Eye Witness to Therapy* by F. S. Perls, copyright 1973, and *Gestalt Therapy Now* ed. by J. Fagan and E. L. Shepherd, copyright 1970.

Macmillan Publishing Co. Inc., New York, *Science and Human Behavior* by B. F. Skinner, copyright 1965, and *Experiencing and the Creation of Meaning* by E. T. Gendlin, copyright 1962.

From *Psychology: A Study of a Science, Vol. 3. Formulations of the Person and the Social Context* ed. by S. Koch. Copyright 1959. Used with permission of McGraw-Hill Company.

Jason Aronson, New York, *The Handbook of Gestalt Therapy* ed. by C. Hatcher and P. Himelstein, copyright 1976.

From *The Farther Reaches of Human Nature* by Abraham H. Maslow, copyright 1971 by Bertha G. Maslow. Reprinted by permission of Viking Penguin Inc.

Oxford University Press, Walton Street, Oxford, *Journals* by S. Kierkegaard, translated and edited by A. Dru, copyright 1938, by Permission.

Psychology Today, Ziff Davis Publishing Co., New York, for permission to quote from D. Goleman interview with Gregory Bateson, copyright 1978.

From *Toward a Psychology of Being*, 2nd edition by Abraham H. Maslow, copyright 1968 by Litton Educational Publishing, Inc. Reprinted by permission of D. Van Nostrand Company.

Real People Press, Moab, Utah, *Gestalt Therapy Verbatim* by F. S. Perls, copyright 1969, and *In and Out the Garbage Pail* by F. S. Perls, copyright 1972.

Brunner/Mazel, Publishers, New York, *The Growing Edge of Gestalt Therapy* ed. by E. W. L. Smith, copyright 1976, and *Creative Process in Gestalt Therapy* by J. Zinker, copyright 1977.

Gary M. Yontef, Ph.D., for permission to quote from his privately published work, *A Review of the Practice of Gestalt Therapy*, copyright 1971.

Gertrude Krause, sole owner of the copyright of her privately published monograph, *Some Notes on Gestalt Therapy Training*, copyright 1977.

W. W. Norton & Company, Inc., New York, *A Theory of Personality* by G. Kelly, copyright 1963.

John Wild, *Existence and the World of Freedom*, copyright 1963, pp 12-13. Reprinted by permission of Prentice-Hall, Inc., Englewood Cliffs, New Jersey.

The Gestalt Journal for permission to quote from an interview with Laura Perls, copyright 1978.

Julian Press, *Gestalt Therapy: Excitement and Growth in the Human Personality* by F. S. Perls, R. F. Hefferline, and P. Goodman, copyright 1951 by Perls, Hefferline, and Goodman. Copyright renewed 1979. Used by permission of Crown Publishers Incorporated.

Foreword

Frederick S. Perls, M.D., completed his seminal work on gestalt therapy, *Ego, Hunger and Aggression: A Revision of Freud's Theory and Method,* in 1939. Four decades later, Vernon Van De Riet, Margaret P. Korb, and John Jeffrey Gorrell have written the first formal text for students in gestalt therapy. Bravo! It is fitting that this book be published in 1980, the tenth anniversary of Dr. Perls' death.

Thirty years ago, Perls, Hefferline, and Goodman published the second major work, *Gestalt Therapy.* Since that time, Perls and others have published several more informal and spontaneous accounts of gestalt therapy, as well as many anthologies. Other authors (such as Polster and Polster, Zinker, and Simkin) have written in depth about gestalt therapy from their perspectives at the time. In addition, "pop psych" books from a gestalt perspective have abounded. In this book, Van De Riet, Korb, and Gorrell, experienced clinicians and scholars, have written a text rich in gestalt therapy and grounded in the academician's respect for rigorous thought. The clinician scholar is all too rare an author in the field of psychotherapy, particularly when his or her presentation is of a specific therapeutic orientation, rather than an overview of many "schools." Psychotherapy is both an art and a science, not franchise for emotional/behavioral anarchy or dogma.

Any approach to psychotherapy must, at the very least, address itself to the crucial issues of philosophy, methodology, and technology. The authors do that and more. They begin by reminding the reader of the scientific method as it relates to theories, theory construction, types of validity, and evaluation of a theory's usefulness. How one organizes one's world is both the beginning of theory construction and a splendid point of introduction to the gestalt therapy approach. The authors provide some of the links between the philosophy of science, theory construction, gestalt perceptual psychology, and gestalt therapy. The existential philosophical assumptions of gestalt therapy are made explicit, as well as the holistic, phenomenological, and dialogic aspects of the gestalt approach. The methodology and goal (awareness and integration) are clearly defined in terms of process: structure and function.

In their discussion of personality theory, the authors acknowledge the great debt that gestalt therapy owes to psychoanalysis, behaviorism, field theory, phenomenology, and existential philosophy. They then go on to describe some of the gestalt therapy lexicon of "psychopathology." Actually, Perls describes neurosis, although not all psychotherapy, as a maturational block in development, and not as a structural deficit. The parameters of the gestalt therapy approach to "pathology" and psychotherapy are more horizontal and more process– and systems–related than the more traditional dynamic, vertical view. What is salient from the past and/or the future has a life in the present, where therapy occurs. Gestalt therapy is grounded in an existential growth model of "dis-ease" and psychotherapy, rather than a sickness/medical model based on biological determinism. Later in the book the authors outline some relationships between the gestalt therapy view of "dis-ease" and the methodological issues involved in dealing with it from a gestalt perspective.

The authors describe the gestalt therapy view of the nature of change (both intrapsychic and inter-environmental), and how the methodology of this approach follows from its hypotheses of *what* can change and *how* change can occur. Specific comments on the issue of how change occurs in psychotherapy are not easy to find in many books in the field.

Although the authors describe the low priority given in gestalt therapy to the use of techniques, sections of the last chapters, if considered out of context, might reinforce the widespread belief that gestalt therapy is primarily a set of techniques. Such a belief is erroneous; those who hold it are misinformed. To value or use any gestalt techniques without an integrated understanding and assimilation of the matrix from which they emerge is to *miss entirely what gestalt therapy is all about*. If every technique that any gestalt therapist had ever used before were never used again, true gestalt therapists would barely be affected. In fact, such a situation would precipitate even more experimentation and creativity at the boundary, at the cutting edge.

Gestalt therapy is a process of creative experimenting, not a procrustean structure. The polarity would be to do *only* fixed techniques and gimmicks, giving birth to therapists who are "gestalt traffic cops," and clients who are "gestalt robots." Gestalt therapy is more than "hot seat dialogues," more than "dream work," more than blanket "frustration," more than *any* codified set of techniques. Gestalt therapy has as its core holistic, phenomenological, existential, humanistic and dialogic elements whose matrix is ignited and grows, limited only by the therapist's background and creative richness. Gestalt therapy is neither a license for a therapist to do whatever he or she wants nor a set of pre-packaged and therefore sometimes plastic techniques. To paraphrase James S. Simkin, Ph.D., a leading gestalt therapist,: *a technique is a freeze-framing of what at its conception was a creative figural leap in a difficult situation.*

Gestalt therapy has always been vitally concerned with the relationship between the human organism and his or her environment, together making up the situation, the whole. To deal with either to the exclusion of the other legislatively denies the reality of the whole, resulting in psychotherapeutic blindness. The developers of gestalt therapy, Drs. Fritz and Laura Perls, as well as other gestalt therapists, have continually experimented with ways to facilitate increased self and world awareness, drawing on their own strengths, resources, aesthetics, and interests at the time. Unfortunately, casual observers with insufficient background, and therapy dilettantes have mistaken their phenotypical behavior of the day for the genotype of gestalt therapy. Hence, there are some self-appointed "gestalt therapists" who, in fact, represent only a lifeless, still photograph (a fixed gestalt) of an ever on-going, pulsating, and changing adventure.

Van De Riet, Korb, and Gorrell emphasize the importance of the gestalt therapist being broadly based in knowledge and experience, as well as being highly trained, and having integrated the philosophical and methodological sub-strata inherent in the gestalt therapy approach. Psychotherapy isn't instant; nor is preparing to be a psychotherapist.

It has been my personal pleasure to write this foreword. The authors are solid; the book is a fine introduction to gestalt therapy. Its publication marks the possible beginning of a new era in the presentation of gestalt therapy to students. Taste, chew, discriminate, and enjoy.

Robert W. Resnick, Ph.D.
Gestalt Therapy Institute of Los Angeles

Preface

Human behavior continues to be an unendingly fascinating territory for students who want to explore, explain, or understand, and for practitioners who want to manage, change, or control. For students of human nature, great questions have been postulated: Who or what is man? What does he know? What can he know? How does he know what he knows? What does he value? What does he believe in? How is belief possible? Attempts of philosophers, psychologists, sociologists, and anthropologists to answer these questions fill libraries and smoke-filled rooms. Great methodologies have been developed to manipulate or control human behavior with mountains of rhetoric, sophisticated offerings in many media, research instruments and practices, and political and religious strategies.

In this book, we are focusing upon the gestalt (wholeness, pattern) orientation to the living of life and to the ways of working with other people who have trouble in living theirs—the gestalt orientation to the practice of psychotherapy and the processes that may be tools for use in effective living. Thus, we are interested in psychological theories, in philosophical assumptions, *and* in change strategies and methods.

In each chapter we shall deal with the totality of gestalt from one particular perspective; that is, from psychological theory, from philosophical assumption, from aspects of clinical practice, from the outside "looking at," or from the inside "experiencing." In the appendix we present a transcript of a gestalt therapy session with our notations as to the kinds of interventions the therapist is making and the therapeutic processes involved. Each of these is a part of the whole and can be dealt with in some measure through our words on paper. The whole, however, is different from the sum of these parts, having, in addition, the quality of wholeness. It can only be experienced personally and immediately and in practice as a gestalt-oriented person or therapist.

Although we quote copiously from Fritz Perls as the primary source of information about gestalt therapy, we make no effort to capture his lusty, energetic, colloquial, and charismatic flavor. The reader is urged to read Perls himself, both for that and for the study of the development of gestalt therapy from origins in psychoanalysis, gestalt psychology, and other sources. Our aim is to answer the many questions our students have asked over the years as they have been stimulated by the power of the system and have wanted more detailed explications of the theory and the practice than they and we found readily available. We hope other students will find our discussions relevant and educational; we expect reactions from you who are stimulated by them in one way or another.

Our position vis à vis the credentialing and training of gestalt therapists may be clear to the reader of this book. However, because we have particular concern, we want to make a statement here. To be a gestalt therapist demands great clarity, self-awareness, and a personal ethical stance as well as insight, technique, and skill. Some of the gestalt techniques are deceptively simple; it is possible to lift them from the body of theory, training, and experience upon which they rest. It is also possible that damage to clients may result when powerful techniques are used without understanding and experience. Training and certification procedures are under scrutiny and, we believe, need to be studied carefully in the light of the increasing interest in this approach to therapy. It is our belief that thorough, reputable training over several years, whether certified or not, is essential for proficiency. A careful reading of this book will indicate why we hold that belief.

Each of the three persons who collaborated in the writing of this book has had a different experience with gestalt therapy. Vernon Van De Riet found gestalt therapy to be profoundly helpful at a time of personal crisis about 12 years ago, and, after that experience, he completed the training program of the Los Angeles Institute of Gestalt Therapy. Since 1970, he has continued to learn and to grow by training others in this discipline. He is currently interested in the integration and use of the gestalt approach with other forms of psychotherapy and other approaches to human growth and change. Through reading a pamphlet brought to her more than 20 years ago from an Esalen workshop led by Fritz Perls, Pat Korb had a "recognition" experience: she knew she had found something for which she had been searching. Ten years ago, she was given the opportunity to explore the gestalt orientation for herself. She took it. During the past nine years she has been actively involved as a student, a trainee, and a trainer. Jeff Gorrell discovered the personal and professional implications of gestalt therapy from the other two authors while enrolled in their advanced training courses. In the past few years, the knowledge gained from association with them has reached into all areas of his professional development.

For all three of us gestalt therapy has provided important and personally satisfying work experiences both as clients and as therapists. All three of us are educators and have been actively searching out the fundamentals so that we may both understand and instruct in the gestalt approach. What we share is our understandings, arrived at through personal and collaborative efforts. We are profoundly grateful to too many persons to name: our family members, colleagues, students, and friends who have supported, challenged, typed, and otherwise helped in loving ways. We are solely responsible for the statements made herein.

Because the gestalt approach is dynamic and we are dynamic persons, constantly in the process of growing and changing, we might write this book very differently tomorrow or next year. We would then know more, have experienced more, and be more understanding of core constructs and experiences. We have stopped the time, made a cross-cut through our experience, and share with you what we know, believe, perceive, and imagine at this time. This is an introduction to gestalt therapy as we experience it and write of it today—October 1979.

Chapter 1
Theoretical Foundations of Gestalt Therapy

Although he sometimes disclaimed the credit, Frederick S. (Fritz) Perls is generally considered to be the primary developer of one of the most powerful psychotherapies to evolve in the twentieth century, gestalt therapy. *Gestalt* is a German word which has no exact translation in English. The closest we come is wholeness, configuration, or completeness of form. The reasons for Perls' choice of this label will be discussed in this chapter, as well as aspects of other systems, including gestalt psychology, upon which Perls drew. However, the system developed by Perls goes far beyond the constituent elements, being enlivened and informed by Perls' genius into a totality of a therapeutic system—a gestalt in itself.

We begin with a discussion of the psychological foundations of gestalt therapy, moving in later chapters to philosophical assumptions, psychodynamics, definitions of health and "dis-ease," change processes and the course of therapy, and the role of the therapist in the process. A demonstration of gestalt therapy in action may be found in the appendix with our comments as to the choice of interventions and the progress of the therapeutic interaction. Let us first look at the nature of psychological theory, and then discuss theoretical perspectives in gestalt therapy.

THE NATURE OF THEORIES

Theories of personality, behavior, learning, and psychotherapy, no matter what their particular orientation or philosophical basis, share some important characteristics. Since theories organize phenomena, they must be considered as tentative conceptualizations, subject to rigorous examination and questioning concerning their adequacy as meaningful systems of thought. Guidelines

1

for assessing the adequacy of a theory have been devised, notably by Gordon Allport (1947). Reporting the results of the Social Science Research Council on the validation of social theory, he lists several necessary considerations: subjective certainty, comparison with existing theory, mental manipulation, predictive power, and internal consistency. Before we look more closely at the characteristics of a valid theory, let us use an experiment to better understand the usefulness of theories.

Imagine that you have been invited by your best friend to take a vacation in the mountains near the village of Eagle's Nest, Colorado. Since this is a fantasy, let us imagine that all expenses have been paid, and that you have a rental car waiting at the airport in Denver, Colorado. You have been told that Eagle's Nest is 90 miles from Denver; however, you do not know what roads to take. Your immediate need is for a road map of Colorado—a map that depicts, in some fashion, the territory of Colorado. You locate Eagle's Nest on the map and plan the route you need to take from Denver.

A theory is, in many ways, like the map of the state of Colorado. It is a map of a territory. As Alfred Korzybski (1933), the founder of general semantics, points out, the map is not the territory; the way we organize and symbolize our experience is not the experience, nor is it the thing we symbolize. For example, using our road map analogy, we can agree that no one is able to travel from Denver to Eagle's Nest on a road map itself. It is a representation, a way of organizing and picturing the territory over which we wish to travel. Likewise, in psychology or in psychotherapy, our theories (or maps) are not the territory. A theory about experience and behavior differs from the experience and behavior itself. However, just as a map is useful in traveling, a theory can be useful. We can increase our ease and efficiency in working; we can avoid routes that take us on sidetracks, and we can choose the best route. If we have a good theory, we are much more likely to reach our goal, much less likely to run into a dead end.

A map does not give us all the necessary information and skill for driving to Eagle's Nest. We need to be in control of our vehicle and to know its operation, its limitations, and its functions. We need alertness and experience to translate the symbols from the map into recognition of the territory as we travel through it. The road map we obtain from the American Automobile Association will be similar to the map we obtain from a local service station, though they may vary in style and complexity. However, the maps we obtain from a geological survey will feature different aspects of the territory. The maps do not negate each other; they have separate functions. In psychology, the theory that we obtain from a behaviorist will be quite different from Freudian, Rogerian, or gestaltist theory. There are many ways of conceptualizing the territory of human experience and behavior.

Returning to Allport's guidelines for evaluating a theory, we see that the first criterion, a feeling of subjective certainty about the theory, underscores the intuitive or organismic side of knowing. In the example above, if you had spent considerable time exploring Colorado before going on the journey, you would have an internal, cognitive map of the state. You might have enough knowledge so that you would not need a service station map, or you might need the map but be able to look at it and find Eagle's Nest easily. Someone who has wrestled regularly, extensively, and vigorously with a body of knowledge develops a "feel" for the material; he maintains a subjective sense of the logicality, the relatedness, the impact, and the adequacy of the total sum of information he has absorbed. Out of this "feel" for the material, the individual is sometimes able to organize his subjective impressions into a logical framework that can be communicated to others. If you have enough knowledge of the state of Colorado, you might be able to make your own map for someone else.

The initial basis for forming the finished product, the map or theory, lies in the intuitive sphere. Does the theory or map make good sense when looked at from the background of one's experience and one's knowledge of the territory? Allport points out that subjective certainty is one sign that suggests a good fit of intuitive knowledge with specific evidence, though it must always be checked against other criteria.

Gestalt therapy is intuitively appealing to many people. Its theoretical foundations come from many perspectives: psychoanalytic and neoanalytic theories, phenomenology, existential thought, Eastern philosophy, general semantics, and many other sources. It presents a synthesis of the dynamics of psychological functioning that leads many people to an immediate, positive response. The rapid growth of interest in gestalt therapy in the late 1960s and the persistence of interest by professionals and laymen today attest to its high degree of subjective certainty.

In passing from intuition to analysis (the process of justifying subjective knowing or feeling states), we must confront existing bodies of evidence to determine if our theory conforms to scientific evidence and known facts. Although it certainly is true that "known facts" are themselves subject to scrutiny and challenge, and there are apparent contradictions and inconsistencies in the available evidence, there is far greater agreement than disagreement, and greater consistency than inconsistency. It is particularly difficult to confront the known facts derived from clinical practice because the person testing an idea or hypothesis in such a setting is also altering the pace and range of interaction, while, at the same time, interpreting the "evidence" according to prior perceptions. Therefore, it always remains a subjective task to build theories and test them in psychotherapy. Given this difficulty, gestalt therapy, like other therapies, accounts for the dynamics of change and growth as perceived by the therapist.

Let us return to our earlier map analogy to clarify Allport's points. Traveling in Colorado would be hazardous indeed, if the map maker decided to leave out sections of the state because he didn't like or understand them, hadn't explored them, or thought they weren't important. Extending our analogy to more closely approximate the difficulties in building theories about human behavior, imagine how much more difficult it would be to draw a road map of Colorado if, when we admired, talked to, walked on, or interacted in any way with the mountains, roads, and villages, they would change in some significant way. Our road map could no longer be a reflection of the territory itself; it would have to account for continual change of all kinds—interaction of the traveler with the terrain and interaction effects that different parts of the terrain might have on each other. In point of fact, these changes do happen in natural surroundings; however, they happen so slowly that maps can be made that are effective guides for travelers. Theoretical maps of the territory of human behavior are more difficult, and creating a theory that takes into account all known facts and evidence becomes not only a challenge but also an obligation (Maslow 1966).

While accounting for the existing evidence and organizing it into a coherent body that will fit into existing bodies of knowledge, one must subject this evidence to mental experimentation, Allport's third criterion. Several steps are important in this stage. First, alternative explanations are to be considered. The body of evidence may be accounted for in several ways, in which case the favored explanation must be validated and the possible alternatives disproved. Such analyses must be intellectually sound and semantically apt. Secondly, levels of analysis are to be extended; that is, the explanation must be applied to other similar phenomena in order to ascertain that it does not apply to them but is localizable to the one phenomenon or body of evidence being considered. In the third place, both short-term and long-term implications of the explanation are to be examined. Such questions must be asked as: Is the explanation limited in scope to only the phenomenon in the present circumstances or can it be legitimately applied to hypotheses of the future? Are the cause-and-effect analyses sound?

Sir Arthur Conan Doyle's (1967) fictional character Sherlock Holmes is an admirable example of a person who at all times practiced powerful processes of mental manipulation. Holmes speaks of an ideal reasoner who can take a single fact in all of its surroundings and from that knowledge deduce the antecedents and also the results that will follow from it. We may note that such precision is possible in literary works of art, while phenomena in the world we experience are neither so discrete nor so easily limited. However, Allport's third criterion involves mental manipulation of the Holmesian variety—both science and art according to Conan Doyle.

The predictive power of any theory, alluded to by Allport must be a major consideration. Allport suggests that this fourth criterion is not sufficient in itself for concluding that a conceptualization is adequate, but if a theory has predictive power or heuristic value, then it is greatly improved. This suggests that the theory of therapy that best predicts growth or change in the client has the best organized conceptualization of personality dynamics. However, given the nature of such recognized phenomena as self-fulfilling prophecies, the predictions made by a therapist concerning any particular client would exert influences upon the behavior of both.

While predictive power can be approached on levels ranging from simple historical/sequential predictions (as in predicting what behavior a person will next exhibit) to highly abstract predictions (as in predicting changes in personality structure or in mental functioning), a valid theory would maintain means of predicting on all levels of analysis. Therefore, in gestalt therapy, situation-specific predictions are often minimized, except where some salient personality dynamics are involved. Long-term use of gestalt therapy techniques should lead to refinement of its predictive base.

Many of the techniques of gestalt therapy are being used by therapists with other than gestalt backgrounds (Rosenfeld, 1978). In fact, many of the gestalt techniques coincide with techniques used in other therapies. Those techniques that are specifically part of the gestalt therapy model, however, stand up well under the scrutiny of therapists from many different persuasions. Although Allport (1947) indicates the danger of "prestige suggestibility," the acceptance of a particular point of view merely because it is commonly held by others, consensual agreement must be acknowledged and considered.

In addition to external considerations of validity, the validity of any theory rests on the internal consistency of the conceptualization. The various elements within a theory should not deny or contradict each other. There should be a wholeness of perspective—a gestalt—that is self-unifying. A central value in gestalt therapy is the integrated wholeness of personality; within that wholeness there are elements, a theory of health, disease, and the dynamics of personality, that should be internally consistent in order to comply with Allport's criteria for validity. To the authors it is clear that Perls did not intend to present a clearly unified theory; however, our study of gestalt therapy and our therapeutic work in it have led us to formulate internally consistent underlying assumptions and some previously unstated theoretical foundations.

A final consideration regarding theories is in order here. Since theories attempt to provide broad, holistic explanations of reality, an individual well versed in any particular theory tends to rely on that theory as a touchstone for understanding. This often leads to confusion over what is conceptualized, what values, beliefs, and prejudices a person has, and what is real. Many people mistake their theory for the truth, rather than seeing the theory merely as one possible way of organizing perceptions. It is not unusual for psychologists to act as if they believe that reinforcement, for example, is a real entity, instead of being only a useful explanatory concept. Others may believe that the id, the ego, and the superego exist, or that the self-concept is more than a person's own theory about herself or himself. As we explained earlier, the map of a territory is not the same as the territory itself. Just as an individual may seek different types of maps depending upon the questions or interests he has, so may an individual rely upon different theories of behavior at different times. Thus, gestalt therapy may be viewed as one possible way to understand human behavior, one which many persons find useful in therapy, clinical work, and counseling.

GESTALT PRINCIPLES

Perls named his therapy approach after the early gestalt psychologists whose conceptions about learning become organizing principles for describing the overall functioning of the individual. Kohler's (1925) research on insight and Wertheimer's (1959) principles of productive thinking stress the importance of understanding the underlying structure of a problem for true learning to occur. The underlying structure or configuration of a situation is perceived as a total organization by the individual; thus, a meaningful gestalt is the individual's personal construction of meaning out of the available field of impressions.

The individual perceives his environment as a total unit of meaning; he responds to the whole of what he sees, and this whole is composed of the stimuli to which he attends directly, and those to which he does not attend, or "background." Focused attention organizes environmental parts into a visual whole, a gestalt that emerges as a figure dominating a field of impressions. For example, the margins and spaces between letters on this printed page help to define the words and sentences. If there were no margins and spaces, it would be difficult to distinguish what had been written. Although the white margins are "blank spaces," they do not have blank functions. They are integral to the perception of the words.

By extending this principle, a gestalt therapist would maintain that each person, as an organism with internal physiological, psychological, and biochemical organizations, exists in the context of his total environment. His "internal" processes do not operate in isolation. Although he varies within himself, he is bound to his environment by the maintenance of further interrelationships. In his environment, he requires nourishment in myriad forms, and he also contributes to the regulation of this larger context through his relatedness with it. He relates to his environment as a whole organism.

Each person is a complex arrangement of figure-ground relationships. A particular movement, such as stretching out one's legs, will bring to the foreground those parts of the body involved. Nevertheless, the parts remain in context. A nose is understandable in the context of a person's face and in its function as a part of the total organism. If it is observed out of context, by itself, it will be different. If we focus upon noses by themselves, see them without their contextual features or functions, they seem rather strange. This phenomenon occurs because of the disparity between awareness of prior contexts and the lack of present context; continual focusing upon something irrespective of its environment leads to caricatures or exaggerated representations of reality. Similarly, in perceiving an individual, we see him as different in different settings. A fresh look facilitates seeing the person *as he is* in the moment that we see him. Or we may see him detached from his present environment based on other contacts, as a stereotype or caricature of what he really is.

His early work with brain-damaged patients led Kurt Goldstein (1939) to an organismic theory of human personality that stresses the psychobiological whole of each individual. A similar conception of behavior underlies much of the original conception of gestalt therapy and remains a theme that resounds through all of Perls' writings. For example, he says:

The organism is a whole. As you can abstract the biochemical, behavioristic, experiential, etc. function and make one your specific sphere of interest, so you can approach the total organism from different aspects, provided that you realize that any change in any sphere produces a change in every other corresponding aspect. (Perls 1972, pp. 167-168)

In gestalt therapy, what an individual attends to is conceived of as being related to organismic need and need reduction. In an individual, needs arise—come to the foreground— and recede progressively as they receive attention. This continuous perceptual process has been expanded upon by phenomenological psychologists as a model of general human functioning (Combs, Richards, and Richards 1975). Once fulfilled, a need recedes from prominence and others emerge to be fulfilled; they, in turn, recede from prominence when fulfilled. In perceptual terms, a person's perceptions at any time will center around the clear image; he will, in effect, acquire blinders, for he will not ''see'' the other aspects of the environment that do not relate to the dominant need of the moment. His behavior will be directed toward the satisfaction of the dominant need.

The healthy formation of gestalten is a continuous process of emerging figures and receding fields. The highest priority need will emerge out of a complex of needs. Once satisfied, each need will recede from prominence, and the ''figure'' that emerged to satisfy it will revert to part of the total field, or background, and another need will emerge leading to a new gestalt. Any change in awareness will result in the destruction of the present gestalt and the creation of a new one.

Since a gestalt is irreducible, it will disappear if divided into components; a division, as an alteration in perception, creates a new gestalt. The act of perceiving is important to the creation of figure-ground relationships. Although in gestalt therapy there is a tendency to describe gestalt formation and destruction as a process that occurs with or without the individual's participation, in fact, the individual is not separable from the formation of gestalten. Personal awareness of the figure-ground relationship is integral to the relation.

In the forming of the complete gestalt, what a person chooses to attend to becomes an ordering principle. Although we may not often be aware of choice, we do choose what will be the controlling figure-ground relationship of situations. For example, if an individual chooses to see a group of people at a cocktail party as being phony or hypocritical, that choice will color whatever is seen and will order all awareness around characteristics that are congruent with that choice. If the same individual decides that these same people are witty, urbane sophisticates, perceptions of their conduct will center around appropriate confirming details. What might be a sprawling, haphazard conversation would differentiate into a spontaneously sophisticated repartee in one frame of reference or into a plotted and planned manipulation of others from another orientation. The mental ''set'' to respond to certain environmental cues organizes our perceptions and our contact with the world.

Perls suggests that if a person applies ''brain power'' to his or her experience of the world and through force of ''will'' constructs a viable reality, he or she succeeds in thwarting the essential experiential modes of being, and his or her ''will'' becomes the organizing focus. Good gestalt formation is spontaneous. It cannot be forced or ''willed'' for it is composed of whatever attention and concentration are brought to the situation, plus the excitement produced in the merging of attention and situation. Any change in the attention will merely produce a different total experience, but not necessarily in ways that a person ''wills.''

In process, in ''good gestalten,'' clarity and openness are common. If there is a problem to be solved, the person may have what Kohler (1925) calls an insight, an ''Aha'' experience. One might describe that experience by saying, ''Something just clicked into place and I knew exactly what to do.'' In solving problems, the formation of a clear and meaningful gestalt produces a solution which is often accompanied by immediate recognition of its appropriateness. Confusion is dispelled. There is no mistaking the experience and its structural relation to the context and to the self. Thus it is that we ''recognize'' clear gestalten; they are right, understandable, and encompassing, and we know them.

The classic example of an ''Aha'' experience is that of Archimedes, who, while he was taking a bath, suddenly realized the nature of mass displacement in water. His recognition of the physical principles that he had been seeking was so powerful that awareness of other events around him disappeared. As the story goes, he leapt from his bath, dashed into the streets without pausing to dress himself, and cried out, ''Eureka!'' (''I have found it!'') The gestalt of that one experience was so clear and encompassing that it eradicated the other possible gestalten.

In the natural gestalt formation process, our needs or desires arrange themselves into clarity and prominence. The only rule they follow is that the most pressing need will determine the clearest figure. Gestalt therapy, thus, denies the existence of a rigid hierarchy of needs. While on the surface this appears as a rejection of Abraham Maslow's (1962) formulation of such a hierarchy, in fact, the two approaches are complementary. Maslow (1954) says that the human being is motivated by a number of basic needs which are species-wide, apparently unchanging, and genetic or instinctive in origin. He is stating an understanding of species' needs, and does not presume to account for an individual's needs at any one time or place. Gestalt therapy does the latter; it accounts for particularized and even idiosyncratic needs as a process of gestalt formation and destruction. Both theories base their systems on "first things first," a self-regulation process.

In gestalt therapy, natural functioning is seen as an ongoing process in which all parts organize into a whole having characteristics and functions not included in any of the parts. The scientific mind, on the other hand, organizes phenomena into constituent parts and develops further theories and concepts about the parts. Perls recognized this tendency to reduce experience unnaturally; however, he believed so strongly in the gestalt approach that he called it more than a mere explanatory device: "Gestalt! How can I bring home that Gestalt is not just another man-made concept? How can I tell that Gestalt is—and not only for psychology—something that is inherent in nature?" (1972, p. 61).

Organismic self-regulation comes out of direct organismic experiencing. People often suppress awareness of sensory phenomena to such a high degree that they find it difficult to regain awareness of even simple sensory experiences. Of course, some of this is highly desirable adaptation. To endure even an hour in a congested, dirty city, one must be able to mask the noise level, shorten one's breath to keep from coughing or choking, tune out exhaust smells, squint one's eyes to filter particles of soot and smog, and ignore the physical discomforts of jostling crowds, halting physical progress, and hard pavements. On the other hand, what is lost in this shutting off of the sensory input is an awareness of those processes that continue even when one is unobservant. Since the human body naturally functions as a whole with all its sensory apparatus mobilized or ready for mobilization, the movement of the organism into unawareness through "switched-off" modes of sensing severely limits the possible experiences one may encounter. Thus, Perls claims that one should "go out of your mind and come to your senses."

Organismic knowing is "nonrational" or "intuitive" rather than intellectual "knowing about." According to Perls:

Intuition is the intelligence of the organism. Intelligence is the whole, and intellect is the whore of intelligence—the computer, the fitting game: If this is so, then this is so—all this figuring out by which many people replace seeing and hearing what's going on. Because if you are busy with your computer, your energy goes into your thinking, and you don't see and hear any more. (1969b, p. 22).

Rationality or intellect is only a part of organismic intelligence. When it is overemphasized—as in moralistic doctrines—it blocks the rest of the organismic intelligence.

This distinctly Eastern way of describing thought rejects "mere" rational thought as striving too hard for control over the environment, including the individual's internal environment, at the expense of simple experiencing. We do not have to ''think'' in order to feel our muscles when we move; we do not have to reason out the colors of trees, sky, and dirt; we do not have to compute the sound of thunder. All these activities and perceptions of them continue regardless of our thinking about them, although we may be so solidly engaged in thinking and talking that we sometimes become convinced that our thinking causes physical phenomena. Physical and physiological experiences are natural and spontaneous in the organism, and, in like manner, intuition is the spontaneous knowing in organismic self-regulation.

HOLISM

When holistic principles of dynamic change are applied to psychological theory and to therapy, one's focus centers on the whole person. This means recognizing not only the individualistic nature of a person's organizing and experiencing of events, but also that each person is more than an add-sum composite of behaviors, perceptions, or dynamics. Indeed, this recognition is central to gestalt therapy. A gestalt is, by definition, a whole that is different from the sum of its parts, having the quality of wholeness. Some therapies and some theories consider only a few elements of the person, disregard the rest, and assume that they are making truly meaningful sense out of that person. This is not so in gestalt theory.

From the gestalt therapy orientation, reductionistic approaches deny too much. They deny the physical in order to see the mental; they deny the internal to look at the external, the obvious to observe the hidden. Holistic approaches affirm the complexity of persons and of events; all relevant dimensions are included. Early in his writings, Perls revised psychoanalysis in order to remove what he saw as faulty attention to isolated psychological concepts. In *Ego, Hunger, and Aggression* (1969a), he proposed an approach to ''replace the psychological by an organismic concept'' (p. 14). In the two decades that followed the original publication of that book in 1947, he succeeded in integrating many aspects of Western psychoanalysis, Western philosophy, and Eastern philosophy into a coherent and far-ranging therapy that attests to its holistic concerns and its wide applicability within and without the therapy situation.

The wholeness of any moment, like the wholeness of a person, is not merely a convenient concept or a psychological point of view. Even though it is important to understand holism intellectually, an intellectual understanding is only a partial one. Gestalt therapy rejects the mere use of logical analysis in therapy and in psychological theory because it has been overplayed in Western culture as the sine qua non of knowing. In this rejection of simple intellectual knowing, great emphasis is placed on the dimension, drawing upon nonempirical evidence and events. While it is easy to reject such methods as being nonscientific or nonempirical, we merely exhibit the Western bias unless we are willing to immerse ourselves in the holistic vision that gestalt therapy embraces.

In *The Field of Zen* (1970), D. T. Suzuki presents the conception of the self as a holistic existence that cannot be divided into parts and separated from the rest of the organism. Suzuki tells the story of the debate between the Buddhist philosopher Nagasena and a Greek King Milinda in which Nagasena, following the scientific method, asked the King to declare what the chariot was in which the King had come to the debate. Was it the wheels, or the body, or the yokes, or some other part of the mechanism? The King had to answer that the chariot, in fact, was none of these parts. The chariot could not be found in enumerating its parts.

The point made by Suzuki is that with pure intellect we can separate the existing elements of things, but in so doing we fail to find what we search for. It is not that the whole does not exist, but that the scientific method of separating into parts captures the parts but not the whole. To understand and experience wholeness and the "whole person" we may not use some of our favorite organizing approaches. Things must be seen as process; answers must not be sought through analysis unless we later synthesize; progress must be revealed as an illusion; words must not be confused with objects. We can hardly realize the extent to which we partition experience, divide and dissect realities, until we begin to change our long-standing orientation toward elementalistic explanations.

PSYCHOLOGICAL HOMEOSTASIS

Self-regulation is a spontaneous, integral part of the organism. In order for something to be spontaneous, it must be natural, participating in situations in terms of themselves and not in terms of external controls or devices. When our organism regulates itself in harmony with our own nature—and this is not easily done—we behave spontaneously and naturally. There is no effort of planning or doing; there is just being.

Gestalt theory assumes that in its "being" the organism reaches a psychological balance. However, given the holistic approach, constant changes in external events and new emerging needs create constant change and make it impossible to remain at a balanced point for long. Nor does the organism "want" to remain balanced. In physiological processes, balance is only momentary; as the dominant need of one moment subsides, the next most predominant need emerges. As Walter B. Cannon (1963) points out, homeostatic processes in the organism maintain biological constancy through complex stabilizing arrangements. It has also been proposed by Piaget (1952) that behavioral repertories develop through a balancing process called equilibration which regularly incorporates new ways of organizing knowledge or behavior with the old, established organization of the individual. Both of these approaches to homeostatic processes underline the fact that life is a constantly fluctuating process, not a matter of reaching completion or termination of activity.

In gestalt therapy we also understand that in most situations people believe in, and strive for, finished products. We like a sense of completion and fulfillment. It is comforting to point to a physical, tangible object as something which we have taken to completion. Early research in gestalt psychology (Zeigarnik, 1927; Ovsiankina, 1928) highlighted the tension that is created by unresolved, incomplete experiences. The individual harkens back to unfinished situations in an attempt to finish them. But a finished product is unchanging, unalterable, and functionally dead; a finished product is something we are through with. As long as we are not finished, we are changing, experiencing, continuing. For example, one would not expect to be done with breathing; a person would not say, "I breathed yesterday, and I don't need to breathe any more" yet we try to establish ourselves in fixed, "finished" psychological molds. When we say, "This is me; I am this, and I will always be this," we try to halt the process, to become a finished product. We identify with a state, a stage of process, in the belief that we have found absolute balance.

If we try to make part of a total process into a "thing," then we destroy the process. For a cogent analogy for the homeostatic process, let us imagine children playing on a seesaw. Two children can arrange themselves in such a way as to be perfectly balanced, suspended in the air at both ends, but it is not interesting to do that for very long. For our fantasy children, the movement is up and down, the alteration of the balance by changing position or pushing harder or easier is more interesting and involving.

Psychologically, when we reside at the balance point, we have our energy available to go in any direction. We can recognize the potential for movement in whatever direction *without investing* in any of the alternatives, or attempting to maintain a still point. Perls, Hefferline, and Goodman call this "creative precommitment":

Note the difference between idling in "neutral," where no force is applied forward or backward, and straining forward with the brakes set. The first is a situation of "resting," while the second is one of extreme conflict . . . . "Creative precommitment" is the indifference-point of a continuum, poised between but *aware of and interested in the potential* situations which extend in either direction. One feels the beckonings to action, but is not yet committed to either side. (1951, p. 44)

A person can be committed to actions without denying the validity or the existence of homeostasis within. While doing something, one may be aware of the freely flowing movement, the adjustments and shifts that are made to accommodate oneself to the world. Someone may see that he or she is engaged in a moment that is part of an unfolding relation with the world. Although attending to the foreground experience, he or she does not neglect the perspective afforded by the whole figure-ground relation. Since balance comes out of active gestalt formation and destruction, attending to foreground experience in those terms is accepting the process of adjustment and balance. He or she can maintain psychological homeostasis only by maintaining a holistic orientation toward process and interaction.

In addition to seeing oneself as being in balance with life processes, the individual may also direct attention to the balance in the world. In fact, self-perception and other-perception are synchronous. Often the aspects that one assumes about the world are also those one assumes and acts upon within oneself. If one believes in the finitude of the universe, one will also believe oneself to be finite. If the world is seen as a series of objects to be manipulated and controlled, self-manipulation and self-control result. If the world is seen as an objective phenomenon, having intangible, empirical qualities, the individual will be perceived in the same way, as a static film clip rather than as a moving picture. Even though the picture is clear, it is static, not alive and vital. The recovery of vitality and liveliness is a pervasive aspect of gestalt therapy (Polster and Polster 1973).

THERAPY ANTECEDENTS

Gestalt therapy shares some basic premises with psychoanalytic, neoanalytic, and humanistic approaches to therapy. One essential agreement is that there is a healing process that may be employed effectively for each individual. A further basis for agreement is that the individual is a complex arrangement of dynamic relationships. Understanding the dynamics of personality, then, is important in order to understand the total person and in order to employ effective therapeutic measures. How these dynamics are treated may vary from therapist to therapist, but a recognition of basic dynamics, such as defense mechanisms, is common to various psychotherapies.

Basic psychoanalytic theory makes several assumptions about personality and therapeutic processes that gestalt therapy shares. The initial assumption is that a person is able to overcome neurotic mechanisms through some form of self-knowledge. That is, in the company of a therapist the individual may bring to awareness past experiences, present emotions, and future intentions in such a way as to overcome neurotic manifestations of personality characteristics. Perls was trained as a psychoanalyst; influences from psychoanalysis are evident in his writings.

While Freud and Perls shared some general perspectives, Freud provided a set of perspectives about human psychodynamics and therapeutic practices against which Perls avowedly sharpened his own perceptions and practices. He differed from Freud in significant ways, as Edward W. L. Smith has pointed out in his essay delineating the roots of gestalt therapy (1976). Paramount differences had to do with Perls' holistic-organismic position, with his adoption of basic gestalt psychological concepts and his use of polarization principles and homeostasis. In therapy; Perls radically departed from psychoanalysis through his insistence on experience (here-and-now awareness), rather than description or discussion (talking about), as the primary mechanism.

Differences from Freud were shared by neoanalysts, who also shared significant concepts with Perls. Foremost among neoanalysts in influence was C. G. Jung, Freud's pupil, colleague, and later foe, who postulated an individuation process occurring throughout life. According to Jung, as the various elements and tendencies of the individual are actualized, that is, as the individual realizes the potentialities of all aspects of the self, the individual becomes more developed, more complete. The self tends to approach the maximum possible differentiation and actualization; the individuation process is the means whereby this is attained. Undeveloped parts of the individual readily become factors that drain energy from the more developed areas of personality, leading eventually to neurotic mechanisms (Hall and Lindzey, 1970). This concern with the limiting effects of under-realized portions of the self also characterizes much of gestalt therapy. In the gestalt system, unrealized aspects of self are "disowned" by the individual, and it is only through the appropriate "re-owning" of these aspects that the individual is able to become truly fully-functioning.

The concept of psychic energy as developed by Jung also is important in gestalt therapy. Jung considered psychic energy as a biologically-based "life energy." Gestalt therapy, too, treats this construct of energy as part of the natural functioning of the organism, but does not relate the concept of energy systematically to the overall structure of personality. Instead, the treatment of energy is more functional, a means of relating the individual's investment in present, past, or future activity. In these terms, investment of energy in unfinished, incomplete experiences draws energy away from present functioning, thus inhibiting the ability of the individual to participate fully in present experiences. Investment of energy in denying aspects or characteristics of the self also drains energy from the ongoing actualization of the individual.

A third significant construct coming from Jung's analytic theory is that of polarity (Polster and Polster 1973). While Jung sees the polarities as aspects of the overt personality having counterparts in the "shadow," the gestalt therapy view is that both poles are balanced in the personality although both may not be in conscious awareness. Any part of the self has a counterpart that is available for knowing and understanding. Thus, gestalt therapy postulates that behind every good little girl is a bad little girl ready to break free, and for every negative emotion there also is a positive counterpart. Allowing expression of the unexpressed or unaccepted qualities within the individual is pervasive in therapy processes. Therapeutic techniques designed to bring into awareness the polarities of experience enable the individual to become more complete and spontaneous.

One of the most spectacular of these gestalt therapy techniques, wherein the individual acts out dialogues between opposing parts or feelings, is related to psychodrama as developed by J. L. Moreno (1946). The psychodrama technique allows the individual to stage a reenactment of an important event or a symbolic enactment of personal feelings or conflicts. In a group therapy setting, members of the group may take assigned parts, representing significant individuals so that the person may gain appropriate release of blocked emotions or awareness of personal dynamics contributing to problems in life. By providing a method of bringing the past into the present and acting out rather than discussing problems, psychodrama contributes much to contemporary therapeutic technique. The value of such role-playing lies in the immediacy of the enactment which transcends elaborate attempts at explaining or justifying behavior. While the gestalt approach concentrates upon internal conflicts and personal projections by having the client assume all of the roles that typically are distributed among members of a psychodrama group, the essential process of bringing experience into the here and now is the same.

From Wilhelm Reich, gestalt therapy adopts the concept of muscular armor (Polster and Polster 1973), wherein the individual is considered to lodge emotional responses in the body's musculature. Unacceptable emotions are repressed through habitual bodily mechanisms, many of which may consist of selectively tightening and restricting muscle groups. In Reichian therapy the actual relaxation of those rigidly protective armors is an essential process in releasing the individual's restricted energy. Perls, like Reich, sees therapy as an integrative act that pertains not only to the psychological world of the individual, but to the somatic world as well. Thus, the sensing body becomes a useful route to psychological awareness in gestalt therapy. Most recognizable of the influences from Reichian therapy is the attention to what the individual is doing physically at the moment, and focusing attention upon the external behavior as an indication of what is occurring internally.

Gestalt therapy owes much of its power to Perls' creative synthesizing of elements of earlier formulations in psychotherapy, as may be witnessed in the above examples. Ultimately, however, as Smith (1976) points out, "Perls' genius was demonstrated . . . in his creation of a new system which in its essence goes far beyond the constituent elements. Gestalt therapy is, in a very real sense, a Gestalt" (p. 3).

RELATIONSHIP TO BEHAVIORISM

As we have seen, the gestalt approach places much emphasis upon and is described as a phenomenological and existential approach to an understanding of man. Even though some of the basic assumptions about man differ, in its concentration upon a person's behavior and in dealing with the obvious, gestalt therapy shares several major points of view with behaviorism. Both state that we must deal with present behavior, that understanding the past rarely leads to change, and that dealing with the reasons for behavior has limited therapeutic value. Both approaches begin by describing what the person is doing as opposed to what the person should do or has done. In the behavioral approach, change occurs through the shaping of behavior by reinforcement, and the control of behavior is seen as primarily outside of the person. The gestalt approach accepts the existence of external reinforcers, but describes change as being initiated by choice based on internal awareness and beliefs rather than external controlling variables. The gestaltist assumes that through awareness of internal processes the individual has a choice of behaviors. The radical behaviorist assumes that external reinforcers are primary, and awareness in itself does not necessarily lead to choice.

In gestalt therapy, we assume that change through personal choice will not occur until the person accepts what is in the present, since verbal responses, modes of action, and habitual ways of perceiving and organizing beliefs often are means of avoiding awareness on the part of the individual. Gestalt therapy interrupts the individual's usual coping styles. Once attention is directed toward awareness of actions, thoughts, intentions, and desires, the therapist directs the client toward a level of knowledge that permits personal choice. The therapist reinforces the client for changing behaviors that block his growth and, in that way, functions as an agent for behavioral change as well as attitude change.

Skinner says that, since behavior "is a process, rather than a thing, it cannot easily be held still for observation. It is changing, fluid, and evanescent, and for this reason it makes great technical demands upon the ingenuity and energy of the scientist" (1965, p. 15). This is true as long as one is observing the individual behavior from the outside. Attempting to control, predict, change, or shape an individual's total behavior is overwhelming; thus, the usual choice of behaviorists is to select small, isolated bits of behavior that are susceptible to external control.

On the other hand, recognizing the difficulties of trying to alter behavior externally, we can approach the problem from the internal perspective. Once we look at behavior as the external realization of people's perceptions of themselves and their world, we can help them alter their own behavior as they choose by helping them to become more aware of their own feelings and beliefs. In this way, people are assumed to have freedom of choice and to be responsible for themselves and how they behave within their personal context.

The contemporary development of an interactionist approach to describing human behavior (Bandura, 1977, p. 10) states that behavior, intrapersonal characteristics, and environmental factors interact with each other. This interaction of three elements can be studied with a view toward understanding the relative strength of each factor in human life. While the radical behaviorist may emphasize the relationship between environment and behavior, the gestalt therapist emphasizes personal awareness as the most significant factor. In fact, gestalt therapy's emphasis on personal awareness focuses the therapy process on personal factors, freedom, responsibility, and choice.

Within the gestalt model, people are facilitated in becoming aware of themselves and of their ways of performing, thus they increase their ability to choose among several alternative behaviors and, thereby, become responsible for whatever they choose to do. In radical behaviorism, awareness is not discussed as a source of decisions, choices, or freedom; it is, instead, presented as neutral. Skinner does discuss self-knowledge in an illuminating chapter in *Science and Human Behavior,* and he comes close to positing internal processes in the human being when he says that "complete lack of self-knowledge . . . can be attributed to the avoidance of the effects of punishment" (1965, p. 366). Similarly, in gestalt therapy, a lack of self-knowledge is seen as an avoidance, controlled by the individual's unwillingness to accept some personal experiences or elements of behavior which do not conform to his or her existing conceptions of self. In its simplest terms, this avoidance leads toward what *appears* to the individual to be a positive end, the maintenance of existing beliefs about the self.

In gestalt therapy sessions, the therapist will often direct the individual's attention to some piece of behavior. When the individual becomes aware of a significant behavior that heretofore has been unknown, he or she can gain from that knowledge. Intellectualizations, "insights," or understanding "why" are usually counterproductive events. Gestalt therapy, like behaviorism, has little interest in producing intellectual "insights," which often have the effect of reinforcing the existing behavior. The gestalt approach encourages the individual first to observe behavior and then to re-experience it directly. Re-experiencing it brings it to the surface, so that the individual can then deal with it directly. Skinner observes that self-knowing is a special repertoire which may or may not be reinforced. Gestalt therapy promotes awareness, and awareness is viewed as something that is reinforced by effective changes.

An important role of the therapist in the gestalt model is to direct awareness toward what the individual is doing to block self-expression of feelings, thinking or action. Since the neurotic is characterized as being blind to the obvious, presenting the client with occasions for focusing upon obvious behavior is, in effect, organizing an opportunity to control one's own contingencies. About the role of awareness, Skinner says, "the crucial thing is not whether the behavior which a man fails to report is actually observable by him, but whether he has ever been given reason to observe it" (1965, p. 289). In these terms, we would say that gestalt therapy, like several other therapies, gives the individual reason to observe behavior, and offers methods for observing, knowing, choosing, and being in charge of it.

SUMMARY

In this chapter, we have looked at the psychological theory within gestalt therapy, and have seen that the conceptual base is holistic with homeostatic and self-regulatory processes. Gestalt therapy incorporates the figure-ground perceptual principles of gestalt psychology and defines motivation in terms of the psychological need to complete gestalten. The learning theory is related to social learning theory (Bandura, 1977) in that people are considered to function and to learn in terms of continuous reciprocal interaction between person and environment. The symbolizing capability and self-regulatory processes of people are of central importance psychologically. Eastern psychological premises of holism and Jung's individuation process are also related, as are the acting/experiencing of psychodrama and the immediacy of obvious behaviors that are the focus in behaviorism.

Chapter 2
Philosophical Assumptions of Gestalt Therapy

THE NATURE OF A PHILOSOPHICAL ASSUMPTION

Psychological theories are useful as descriptions of the complexities of human experience, as chapter 1 has indicated. They are one kind of map of the territory of experience. Maps, however, are based upon assumptions which will now be considered from a philosophical perspective. In some frames of reference any attempt to conceptualize or to theorize is to philosophize. Generally, however, as Suzanne Langer (1957) has pointed out, to philosophize is to deal in some way with the assumptions upon which any theory of man is based; the assumptions themselves about the nature of man, the nature of the environment, and the nature of the interaction between them place the theorist in a historical-cultural context.

In order to understand the nature of the interaction between a theoretical statement and the philosophical assumptions on which it is based, let us imagine a writer who is a psychologist. This imaginary writer comes at some point in his study and experience to a particular understanding of one of the complexities of human life. He desires to communicate his understanding to others. In order to describe the particular phenomenon he has come to understand, he gives it a name. Let us say, just for our purposes, that he labels his understanding the "Maypole Principle." He writes an essay noting the aspects of life that the "Maypole Principle" may describe, and may conclude his essay with a statement such as: "The 'Maypole Principle' is a hypothesis that could prove to be one of the most important evolutionary hypotheses that human beings have ever devised for themselves."

Here, our hypothetical author makes a statement that carries his argument from the psychological arena into a broader context, a philosophical one. The statement indicates that, in addition to being descriptive, the "Maypole Principle" may be good for people—important for all time—and underneath the statement are philosophical assumptions about humankind that are not expressed. The "Maypole Principle" has been devised for the sake of argument. However, other statements in clearly enunciated psychological arguments may be treated in this way; that is, the reader may discover that the deep structure below the verbal statements includes assumptions about humankind, the world, and the nature of the relationship between them. Such assumptions, when lifted from the psychological context, may denote the philosophical "school" to which the author owes some allegiance.

In the case of the hypothetical author of the "Maypole Principle," the clear-eyed student may see that he assumes that human beings are creators; they devise ideas about themselves; they can change; humans evolve—that is, they change in patterned directions. The author does not believe in absolute truths about living; rather, he believes in two things simultaneously: on the one hand, people have free will, can make choices about their lives, can devise significant ideas about themselves; on the other hand, they evolve in patterned ways that are predetermined, over which they have no control. The quoted statement gives no indication as to which of these perspectives might be more central for him.

In the above discussion two philosophical issues have been uncovered: free will vs. determinism and absolute "Truth" vs. changeable truths. Resolution of such issues defines philosophical "schools."

This chapter, then, deals with the assumptions that underlie gestalt therapy, particularly those assumptions that deal with three philosophical issues. First, what is real? What is life? What is the world? In philosophy, these questions fall within the area known as ontology. Second, What is truth? How do we know what we know? These questions define an area known as epistemology. And third, What is good? What is right? What is wrong? This area is axiology. The assumptive answers given in this chapter will be those derived from the gestalt perspective.

THE NATURE OF REALITY

"The Western world begins by making splits, then drawing boundaries, then solidifying those boundaries," according to anthropologist Gregory Bateson (1978). In his statement, there is a basis for gestalt considerations about life, the world, and reality. A "Western world" philosopher such as Bateson describes makes a basic assumption that humankind, the world, life itself can be defined by creating lists of characteristics, traits, or objects, each of which is separate and distinct from each of the others. He then creates sets of categories into which the characteristics, traits, or objects may fit, and describes what is real according to these categories.

A philosopher who espouses the gestalt perspective does not begin an exegesis with sets of objects or categories, but with the assumption that the nature of reality—of life, humankind, and the world—can most profitably be regarded in terms of an ongoing, constantly changing process. There are persons and things; they are recognizable; they exist; they do not exist as static objects or as collections of characteristics. Any aspect of the world is an event, a phenomenon, a performance happening in the immediacy or each moment. These events or happenings are primary phenomena; their primary feature is that they happen and then are gone, transformed by the incoming new elements of the ongoing process.

Objects of which the world seems to consist (such as chairs, cups, books, tools) are processes. First of all, they are combinations of small processes; they consist of molecules, atoms, electrons—moving, shifting, whirling constantly, changing positions. That these miniscule processes cannot be seen without special equipment attests only to the lack of differentiation in the senses. With the help of special equipment, ways have been and are being devised to penetrate and to pass through a supposedly solid "object," with x-rays or lasers, for example.

Viewing these same objects, people, chairs, cups, books, and tools objectively, they may be understood according to their functional processes, their overt ways of participating in events. Chairs are mainly used for sitting, sometimes for alternative activities, but in any event are conceived as part of the process that is going on, and as changed and changing in the process. Cups can contain liquid or solid. Their functions as containers are basic to their existence. Books are read, tools are used in various ways to join, separate, or hold other "things."

A process existence may be recognized in other phenomena. For example, fire is a process of consuming or transforming matter into energy, of producing heat and light. Fire may be described as if it were separate from "things," but, patently it does not exist except as a relation between other processes. It would not proceed without combustible materials such as oxygen. Fire as an observable process is more spectacular than a chair as an observable process, but they are essentially the same with the differences accruing out of their duration, their intensity, and their observable qualities, as well as their physical and chemical makeup.

Sometimes it becomes convenient in a process orientation to note an object as an entity that may exist in its recognizable form. However, in general, gestalt therapists assume that this condition of existence is not possible. All things exist in relation to some other thing or things and, as long as they do, they are engaged in a process. The process, the relation, defines what and how an object is; thus, the characteristics of "things" as processes constitute their existence; the main features are change, flow, mutability, and "happening."

THE ESSENTIAL NATURE OF BEING HUMAN

The nature of being human also falls in the area of ontology, but we will address it separately because of its importance in our argument.

In the gestalt perspective, people are collections of processes; ongoing and changing physiological, emotional, intellectual, psychological, and spiritual processes constitute the existence of each human being. The philosophically operative word in the last sentence is "existence." The stance toward life known as existentialism is one of the solid building blocks in the gestalt approach.

Existentialism has often been characterized in an oversimplified way by the phrase, "What is, is" or, behaviorally, by "How you behave is how you behave," "What you do is what you do," "A rose is a rose is a rose." Generally, existentialism emphasizes that things are not created, maintained, or changed by some inner essence, or by their abstracted qualities or properties. They create, maintain, and change through the simple fact of their existing.

Gestalt therapy aligns itself with the existential stance in denying the categorical approaches to human behavior and embracing the process approach. By attending to processes underlying the concretions of experience, a human being can discover his essential structures of living. Concrete events are important; they are what happens as we perceive our world. A human being's world is constituted by his perceptions of concrete events. Abstract formulations or ideas about events are maps of the concretions, ways of organizing events.

Kierkegaard (1944), the pillar of existentialism, shunned abstract approaches and rejected formulating a general theory of "being." Instead, he concerned himself with what a person does in a real situation. The confrontation between the person and his environmental situation distinguishes him. Kierkegaard saw this confrontation as primal, not separable from what the person is or who he is. The gestalt approach, similarly, maintains that it is the contact between the person and his environment that defines the person's identity. That contact defines the "ego boundary," the limit of the elements that are experienced as "me" and those that are experienced as "not me." That contact is constituted by awareness, which is at the core of gestalt therapy. In existentialism, awareness would be "knowing," for the combination of "knowing" and "knowing about" actively engages the individual in living. Active engagement at the "ego boundary" enables the person to be aware of his world or to "know" it, to be alive.

In speaking of man as living at the ego boundary, psychologists often see and describe these living processes from the perspective of the individual. In the gestalt perspective, however, an individual cannot exist alone; each individual exists within an environmental field with which he must engage (into which he must "aggress," according to Perls (1969a) in order to live. He must engage with the objects of his world in order to survive physically: he must have food, clothing, and shelter, or the resources for providing them; and he must engage with persons in his environment in order to survive psychologically. Man, then, is both an autonomous individual person and an environmentally oriented person who needs other persons, other social institutions. Both the individual and the environment must be affirmed, studied, and described; and the interaction between them must be affirmed, studied, and described. Based on enunciations of Emile Durkheim (1912), some sociologists (cf. Zijderveld 1970; Simmel 1955; Mead 1934, 1962) discuss social phenomena from the *homo duplex,* perspective; i.e., woman or man as both an individual, unique phenomenon and also as a participant in the social roles imposed by the culture (Zijderveld 1970).

Perls (1973) speaks in a similar vein:

No individual is self-sufficient; the individual can exist only in an environmental field. The individual is inevitably, at every moment, a part of some field. His behavior is a function of the total field, which includes both him and his environment. The nature of the relationship between him and his environment determines the human being's behavior . . . . The environment does not create the individual nor does the individual create the environment. Each is what it is, each has its own particular character, because of its relationship to the other and the whole . . . the environment and the organism stand in a relationship of mutuality to one another. (Pp. 15, 16, 17)

In addition to affirmation of both individual and environment, the central gestalt perspective focuses on the interaction process. *How* does a human being interact with his environment? Here, the perceptual psychological processes described in chapter 1 come into play. For the purposes of this chapter, however, examine the existential assumption that underlies these psychological processes: the living processes are those that are dealt with as they exist, as they are. Often, people, particularly philosophers and psychologists, experience the world and themselves in one way, but think about it or describe it in other ways. Kierkegaard in his *Journals* (1938) says, "A man's thought must be the building in which he lives—otherwise, everything is topsy-turvy" (p. 156). In a famous example, he compares the separation of living and thinking to a man building a magnificent castle but leaving it empty and residing in a deteriorating lot next to it. Likewise, according to gestalt principles, "thinking about" removes the person from the "here and now," from the experience of aliveness and engagement, it takes him away from awareness of what is happening. For Kierkegaard, thinking equals detachment, a lack of contact with the world. This is often useful for examining philosophical assumptions, as we are doing in this chapter; however, by thinking alone, we may create unworkable, even spurious, forms for our lives.

Thus far, the philosophical assumptions discussed are: first, the process nature of all of life; and second, the primacy of existence. The third assumption has been alluded to: people observe the events of the world and from that observation create order, structure, meaning, or relationships. The activity of perceiving is a process; it requires an observer and something that is observed, neither of which exists without the other. This is not to say that things do not exist except as they are observed, but that the process of observing in and of itself requires a relation between the observer and that observed, just as "objects" require a relationship with other objects in order to exist.

In viewing man as the creator of his order, his structures for living, the gestalt therapist aligns himself with phenomenologists such as Heidegger (1955). Heidegger postulates a "Being" out of which man's being (being in the world) is created: "Being" is the inner light through which we become aware of our meaning, of what is reality for us. In gestalt therapeutic work, the client is the sole arbiter of his world; "knowing" what is true for himself at any moment is the only valid basis for the ongoing therapeutic process. A therapist may suggest experiments for a client to try—sentences to say, body movements to make, or images to explore; however, the client alone "knows" what words fit, or what the images signify, or what feelings fit the movements. Thus, we see that the gestalt therapist assumes the centrality of a "knowing" self, the centrality of the "being" of man, in Heidegger's terms. A person does not put together an elaborate theory of the self or develop sets of descriptive categories or terms. The person simply "knows" that it is there.

In being the arbiter of reality, then, the self or "being" serves as the center for individual choice, as it is for awareness and attention. When a client experiments with some suggested words or movements and then says, "Yes, this is true for me," a choice is made. The gestalt therapy approach affirms the aware person as the "chooser" of his or her own responses. With awareness comes the possibility of choice. Further, with the choice comes responsibility ("response-ability"). Essentially, each person is responsible for personal choices whether they are made with awareness or not. When choices are made with awareness, however, the "knowing" self, the "being" of each person is engaged.

Each of us, then, acts in and on the total man/environment field by choosing what we will and will not do, what we will accept, reject, think, or feel. It is this choice that makes each of us a responsible human being, in the gestalt view. To quote Perls (1973): "Awareness of and responsibility for the total field, for the self as well as the other, these give meaning and pattern to the individual's life" (pp. 49-50).

The philosopher/psychologist Abraham Maslow (1962) delineates a similar position when he notes man as "transcendent." He calls us to the "clear recognition of [man's] transcendence of the environment, independence of it, ability to stand against it, or adapt to it" (p. 169). For Maslow, there is an "autonomous self" which interacts with the environment in receptive or masterful ways. Autonomy of choice predominates in Maslow's conception, as it also does for the gestalt therapist.

We see, at this point, that the gestalt therapist affirms individual existence, the environment, and the interactive processes between. It is assumed that the individual is autonomous, the creator of his or her own world view. Gestalt therapy assumes the process nature of man, of the environment, and of the interaction. However, we must look at one further factor in the process.

The key factor in the process of constructing reality is that each person is able to represent or symbolize any parts of the world. There are two aspects of this process: first, all parts of the world are interlocked and have resemblances that can be represented or symbolized (Kelly 1963); and, second, human beings are symbol-making and symbol-using/misusing animals (Burke 1966; Cassirer 1946, 1955). Philosophers of language note verbal symbols. Cassirer (1946) describes the process of "noticing" as being animal in nature, function, and direction. To the "noticing" process man adds the process of "denoting" or naming, thereby transforming the physical world into an abstract, conceptual world, a world of ideas and meanings. Denoting or naming is the function of language.

For the gestalt therapist, language is only one of the means of symbolizing experience. We symbolize our experiences in several other ways—through the movements and postures of the body, through images, and through dreams. Symbols may be verbal or nonverbal (Korb 1975). For example, let us explore the following common experience. You are in your home when the telephone rings. You hear the immediate sound of the ringing; your sensory apparatus allows the data of the sound into your ongoing process of awareness. The data are monitored by your intellectual apparatus; that is, you think, "that may be my friend Sam calling." Your thought prompts your physical apparatus to react: you walk to the telephone, pick it up, and say "Hello." Your friend Sam speaks to you and you listen. As you stand listening, you see in your mind's eye the image of your friend Sam, and you smile. You are aware of feeling warm inside. The warm feeling is translated by your intellectual apparatus into gladness. You say, "I am glad you have called!" Here, in this unexceptionable experience, we may note the symbolizing processes that are both verbal and nonverbal. The body feels warm and moves as you symbolize your inner experience. The words symbolize the inner experience. The image in your mind's eye symbolizes your inner experience. These are tools in creating reality, an ongoing process.

There is no proof that the world is a process and not a thing. There is no proof that existence is primary in the experience of humankind. There is no proof that humankind created the world in which they live through their own perceptions and psychological processes. The assumptions, however, are powerful ones, integral and pervasive parts of the philosophical gestalt map of the existence and experience of human beings.

TRUTH AND THE BASIS FOR KNOWLEDGE

Epistemology, one of the main disciplines within philosophy, is concerned with the nature of knowledge. Valid knowledge is presumed to maintain the structure of existence through whatever means of communication may be available. Since gestalt therapy is a discipline and a theoretical system relating human growth and change to personal perceptions of the world, the basis for firm and valid knowledge of the world becomes important.

Gestalt therapy approaches the problem of valid knowledge in nontraditional ways. In traditional Western epistemology, certain knowledge is believed to exist apart from man's awareness of it. It is assumed that ''meaning'' exists and can be grasped, that communication about something can be true, that cause and effect apply in knowledge-seeking, and that knowledge can be analyzed. In gestalt therapy, these assumptions are challenged, and a different orientation toward valid knowledge emerges.

First, the gestalt therapist believes that absolute and certain knowledge is a myth. When we realize the multiordinality of existence, we see that no things are exactly like other things. Everything is different in some unique ways from every other thing. Perceptions of similarity and comparison are invented. Comparison does not exist outside the human framework, and without comparison certain knowledge is impossible. The existing ''knowledge'' of the world is largely based upon such statements as this is bigger than that, less differentiated than those, better than this, more red than that, etc. When we compare, we establish relations. These relations come from the individual.

The traditionalist further assumes that there is a meaning in things, that a meaning exists. Perls (1972) denies both:

A meaning does not exist. A meaning is a creative process, a performance in the here and now. This act of creation can be habitual and so quick that we cannot trace it, or it can require hours of discussion. In every case a meaning is created by relating a figure, the foreground, to the background against which the figure appears. (Pp. 64-65)

In these terms, all that we can *know* about a thing are the relations we perceive. As relations are perceived, they are expressed as clearly as possible in language. However, verbalizing carries with it the assumption that a verbal statement about something can be true, that the speaker's belief in the truth of a statement can be ''justified.'' The criteria for justifiability of belief are based on verbalization of truth: (1) the statement must be true, (2) the person must believe that it is true, and (3) the belief must be based upon adequate evidence that it is true. However, the process of making a statement about something obscures the thing itself through overgeneralization, selective reporting, out-and-out lying, and so forth. Korzybski (1933) says that the act of describing an event inevitably falsifies it. Perls agrees: Gestalt therapy operates on this assumption, that ''verbal communication is a lie.'' Verbal communication is a report of an experience; it is not the experience itself. It is a map of the territory of experience.

The structure of most of our everyday discourse suggests that cause and effect operate in the world. Although it is difficult to conceive of total randomness in the world, it is equally false to believe that knowing *why* something exists is, in fact, knowing that thing. All events are overdetermined, and the line of inquiry that leads to causes for the effects must either dissipate into endless causes or mislead by leaving out causes. Knowing why does not necessarily help in "knowing." If we try to explain current behavior by means of past behavior, we run the risk of endless explanations, speculations, and interpretations. All of those exist; we do explain, speculate, and interpret. However, such verbalizations cover up or are removed from the real experience. To know the experience itself, we must focus upon *how* we feel and not *why* we feel. Knowing *how* is the intelligence of the organism.

In gestalt therapy, organismic knowing is not merely constituted by the intellect, which searches for meanings and for causes. The firmest ground for experience lies in the individual's awareness of bodily sensations (Levitsky and Perls 1970). Gestalt therapy is founded on this concept. As a person becomes aware of body feelings and sensations, she or he bases awareness and choice firmly in the present process of experiencing and being.

The gestalt therapist recognizes that "laws" of behavior are abstractions developed to explain various patterns and processes that have been observed. The gestalt therapist also understands that behavior may have consequences. However, he also understands that there is not necessarily an intervening "reason" for either the consequences or the behavior. Patterns, processes, and events can be recognized and dealt with without analyzing them.

Intellectual knowing also assumes that knowing can be approached analytically, broken into its component parts, and organized categorically. Knowledge, however, in the sense of awareness of organismic "knowing" occurs integratively, not analytically. A person grows, matures, increases, and becomes more whole as he integrates (accepts and assimilates) parts of himself and perceptions of his world.

Gestalt therapy has many links with Eastern thought, as we have noted. One of these emerges from our discussion of the two ways of "knowing." An understanding that encompasses all things at one time is not subject to time and place limitations; this understanding is convergent and synchronous, sometimes beyond words and eluding description. In Zen understanding (Suzuki 1970), this is *prajna*, or intuitive knowledge. There is also the *vijnana*, or discursive knowledge. *Vijnana* is used to describe, separate, analyze, and compute. *Prajna* is used in grasping the totality of an experience. Perls makes a similar distinction between intellectual knowing ("the whore of intelligence") and organismic knowing ("the whole of intelligence").

As we noted in the discussion of gestalt psychology in chapter 1, Kohler and Wertheimer emphasize the integral experience of recognizing the structural relationships in the whole of a problem. In the system of General Semantics Alfred Korzybski distinguishes the thing-as-it-is from the thing-as-it-is-described. Martin Buber's (1958) theological/philosophical perspective offers the I-Thou interaction and the I-It interaction, as do philosophers Merleau-Ponty (1969), Husserl (1970), and others. Kierkegaard (1944) says that it is the totality of the existential encounter, awareness, and choice that are most important and meaningful, most creative of the individual. The ethical stance of Fletcher (1966) and others, as we shall see later in this chapter, proposes a holistic view of interactions and personal responsibility.

In short, the theoreticians and practitioners referred to in this chapter bring to their understandings the holistic view, the oneness or situationality of experience. This view, in one of its oldest forms, is expressed in the Taoist document, the *I Ching* (Wilhelm-Baynes translation, 1950). As C.G. Jung states in the Introduction to the text, the wholeness of the experience of an observed moment includes everything, no matter how small or seemingly insignificant, no matter how great or powerful. Such an approach reflects the Eastern notion that all ingredients of a moment may encompass a philosophy of life, a weltanschauung, which may be transmitted in a therapeutic interaction as, perhaps, the integral, although often unstated, aspect of this interaction (Naranjo 1970).

A review of our discussion of the epistemology of gestalt therapy indicates that all of the elements interpenetrate. That this is true suggests that knowing is a gestalt, a pattern, an irreducible phenomenon. As an experience, it cannot be parcelled, bifurcated, analyzed, subsumed, detailed, explained, or ordered in advance.

HOW A PERSON KNOWS

How a person knows is also an epistemological issue that needs focused attention. For the gestalt therapist, a person knows what he knows as he is aware of his own experience. His awareness becomes the basis for his choices and actions. When gestalt therapy places awareness in one of the key places in its therapeutic system, it links itself with the philosophical movement known as phenomenology, the ''science of experience.'' A person can be aware of the experience of living, which arises from the mutual existence and interaction between that person and his environment.

Gestalt therapy's phenomenological orientation can be related to the writings of Husserl (1970), generally considered to be the founder of the phenomenological movement, and his dictum that things are as they are, not as they are dissected and analyzed. Husserl's conception of the *lebenswelt,* the field of lived experience, is a key factor also in gestalt conceptualization. The *lebenswelt* is ''the world into which we are born, in which we learn our mother tongue and the ways of our culture, in which we may become responsible for our chosen projects, and in which we face death . . . a life world in which we ourselves, our acts and intentions, and all their manifold ranges of objects have their being'' (from Wild 1963, pp. 12-13). For Husserl, the *lebenswelt* is a ground in which each ''I'' exists, as for the gestalt therapist, the world of lived experience is the here and now in which the person exists and from which figures emerge into awareness. Many details of existence are not accessible to the logic and the objective methods of the natural sciences, but can be open to the radically different methods of phenomenology—the disclosure of the world through description or notation of the immediate data of experience as emerging needs bring them into awareness.

It is at this point that the epistemological position already discussed fits into the phenomenology of gestalt therapy. The subjective world of a person's experience is the major component of that person's life and the source of personal knowledge. What is "known" is the derived product of sensory input, structural formation and inner experience. It is not that the structures of the mind are automatically invalid, but that the sensory awareness that is necessary for aliveness has been lost when one is aware only of thinking. The sensory input, the structures of the mind, and the organismic knowing all exist; awareness of them, and of the experiential shift of focus among them, is the natural organismic state. This may be related to Husserl: the here and now is the *lebenswelt,* the life world as it is experienced. The self "knows" as it creates meaning. Through awareness, "the point of contact where being and consciousness meet," the individual experiences aliveness and creates his reality. Although reality is called a "sum of all awareness," it is important to understand that this is not merely an add-sum situation. Experience called "reality" is a here-and-now completeness, an "irreducible phenomenon," a gestalt.

ETHICAL CONSIDERATIONS

Another issue arising out of the existential/phenomenological stance concerns man's relation to man. This question is dealt with in philosophy under the heading of ethics, a branch of the discipline called axiology which deals with moral and value issues.

To ask the questions with which this section is headed is to put ethical issues into a nongestalt orientation. To ask what is right and what is wrong is to assume that there is a right and a wrong, a good and a bad in the matters being addressed. In gestalt therapy there is no "right" or "wrong" built into any matter or question. There are rights and wrongs, but they are aspects of the stance and choices of an individual or of a society in particular situations; their rightness or wrongness is a factor of attitudes and values vis à vis the issues; they emerge in the process of interaction of the person with the environment or of the societal environment with the person.

The gestalt therapist does assume that there are "good" things for each individual, that each individual has values and a valuing process. The therapist also assumes that there are social "goods" and values. These values have their origins in the self, in the culture, and in aspects of the social environment, particularly the family. The individual, however, in the gestalt system is assumed to be responsible for increasing awareness of his value system and, based on his awareness and attention, his choices. We shall return to this issue in later discussion.

The important point is that the "good" things in the gestalt system are not actions; rather, they are attitudes that are to be encouraged as a gestalt way of life. Naranjo (1970) has discussed these attitudes cogently as "moral injunctions" or "general principles." He proposes these three, which we paraphrase here:

1. The valuing of what is actually present in time and space, and real rather than a symbol of a reality.

2. The valuing of personal awareness and the affirmation of personal experience.

3. The valuing of personal responsibility, which constitutes wholeness.

It is not that the gestalt therapist preaches these principles to his clients in the sense of demanding acceptance, nor is it that he holds them as covert injunctions withheld by design. Rather, these principles are statements of "truth" for him and are implicitly supported in all of his work. They represent the "good" for him. Clients who work in the gestalt way are experiencing these "statements of truth" implicit in the therapeutic procedures and processes. Naranjo suggests that success in therapy relates to experiential assimilation of such implicit *weltanschauung*.

To continue with the overt ethical aspects of gestalt therapy, let us consider those that have been enunciated in western culture and philosophy, and explore gestalt therapy's connection with them. Traditionally, only two ethical stances have been stated—the legalistic view, in which laws are considered the controllers of individual decisions and actions (i.e., society is more important than the individuals that live within it); and the antinomian or anti-law view, in which spontaneity or nature controls, and there are no assignable principles. However, there is a third viable ethical stance, whose historical roots go back to ancient China. Confucius, in his *Analects,* wrote, "The superior [wise] man goes through life without any one preconceived course of action or any taboo. He merely decides for the moment what is the right thing to do" (in Watts 1970, pp. 177-78).

Such an ethical stance is noted by Fletcher (1966) as "situation ethics." This system combines the basic ingredients of both of the traditional ethics: authority exists, nature exists; these are interlocking, even inseparable, aspects of any experience. What controls is the individual whose responsibility is grounded *in* each situation. There is no intrinsic right or wrong in any event or in any person. Persons are not intrinsically good or bad. Each person is as he or she is in each situation, and makes choices based upon personal awareness, abilities, knowledge, values, and beliefs. A choice may be made for oneself, for others, or for society. That is each person's inevitable choice.

Fletcher explains the situationalist position as that in which there are players, and there is a game with rules such as "Punt on fourth down" or "Take a pitch when the count is three balls." The wise players know all the rules thoroughly, and also know when to ignore them. For the gestalt therapist, also, there may be some "rules" and there is the breaking of them.

The difficult ethical questions deal primarily, of course, with situations with other persons (although in recent times, dealings with aspects of our environment and of our society have also come to have significance on an ethical level). A central question for us to consider is "Am I my brother's keeper?" Clearly, in gestalt perspectives, the situation controls the persons within the situation. There is no clear yes or no answer to the ethical question as stated. This is not to say that "I" am *not* my brother's keeper, only to say that "I" have the choice and the responsibility for the choice as to attitudes and actions in any specific context.

One further comment related to this ethical stance is necessary for clarity. There is some sense in Fletcher's discussion in which the person may be considered to arrive at each situation without any preconceived ethical attitudes or values, as if all such aspects of interactions were derived from the interaction itself. The gestalt perspective, as we have seen, would include the value systems of the persons; each person has attitudes and values that are brought to any encounter. Part of the therapeutic encounter might involve becoming clear about what attitudes and values are the person's alone and what attitudes and values have been "introjected" (swallowed whole).

Here, a distinction made by Erik Erikson (1964) is helpful. Erikson distinguishes between "ethical" and "moral." In his view, "moral" is legalistic, and he would propose that we consider *moral rules* of conduct to be based on a fear of threats. In contrast, he would consider *ethical rules* to be based on inner processes of judgment and consent and "some promise of self-realization." Morality, in other words, is imposed by external authority; ethics is self-regulation. Each person is considered to have a set of ethical/moral standards that have been developed over many years and which are brought to any encounter. With these, this individual negotiates ethical issues within the emerging situation.

Kierkegaard (as discussed in Wild 1966, Chap. II) also denotes the ethical life as that which continuously chooses the whole of itself, and stands by this choice. This is the authentic existence. Unauthentic existence is detached, and views itself as one object among many others; choice is suppressed.

Carrying this argument back to the *homo duplex* position enunciated earlier—the individual is both uniquely individual and societally bound—individual ethical stances are seen to relate to both individual and societal issues. Persons have values for themselves and for their environments. Some of their "goods" are related to persons and some to society and societal institutions. Persons also have a set of values related to the kind of interaction they favor between the individual and the environment, both other persons and other societal aggregates. The gestalt perspective says that what is "good" about these values and ethics is that they be self-selected, based on personal awareness and choice.

Now let us see what is meant by "authenticity" in the actuality of interaction processes. Martin Buber's (1958) conception of the I-It and I-Thou relationships is central in this respect. Buber distinguishes between two essential processes of relation, the I-It and the I-Thou. In doing so, he ties the two processes to each other, expressing their ultimate need for each other. The I-It process exists in time and space, separating the identities of the I and the It. The It may be either person or object. The important aspect of the process is that the images the I obtains from the It come from distance from it, standing outside it, and observing. The relationship is static. In gestalt terms, this is the intellectual function. The intellect computes, categorizes, judges, weighs evidence, organizes, and so forth.

In gestalt therapy, as in Buber, this intellectual function is seen as an integral part of organismic functioning; however, when used exclusively or overemphasized, this function removes the individual from contact with more direct experience, aliveness. Buber uses the words "experiencing" and "using" to describe the essential processes. "Experiencing" for him is external perceiving of the otherness of the object (person or thing); "using" is treating it as a thing to be manipulated to lead to some result. Although we need to encounter our surroundings in this way, encountering *only* in this way will lead to separation, alienation from what is.

I-Thou relations are those in which I do not encounter objects; rather I encounter other I's. Such encounters occur in interaction between the subjectivity of each I; they do not happen within one or both of the individuals involved. The French philosopher Merleau-Ponty (1969) also suggests this quality of knowing and encountering that reaches such a height of subjectivity that it becomes a new "objectivity," a holistic experience that denies no parts, leaves out nothing.

The language for I-It relations is the daily syntax and the daily words describing daily experiences, past or future imaginings, "talking about" such experiences. I-Thou relations may be articulated but are beyond description. In any event, the description of an I-Thou experience is invalid, for the experience stands outside of descriptive language.

Having outlined I-It and I-Thou relationships, Buber enunciates the ethical position: both stances are necessary; both are valid; one cannot consider either as right or wrong per se; one considers the stances within situations in which one finds himself. For both Buber and Perls, the I-It is the traditional, typical, mechanistic way of relating to aspects of the world. The I-Thou is centered in realization of the self and is, therefore, attainable less frequently.

Perls echoes this ethical stance in his "Gestalt Prayer" which may be found in its entirety in *Gestalt Therapy Verbatim* (1969). When he makes statements that clearly differentiate one person from another and says that each has responsibility for only the self, not for the other's behavior; furthermore, when he indicates that he believes that neither needs to live up to the expectations of the other; and when he defines this kind of statement as a *Prayer* he is often accused of being antinomian—unprincipled and immoral. However, there are ethics within gestalt therapy that are implicit, partially explicit, in the statements. Gestalt therapy emphasizes the importance of "I and Thou; Here and Now." Whatever exists and can exist does so only in the present; experiences of human interaction of the I-Thou kind happen only in the present. Existence and experience, however, are not amoral or immoral. Human choices and decisions are made in every moment. Moral principles are acted out in every lived experience out of the ethical stances of the persons involved. Both I-It and I-Thou experiences are necessary; both are ethical in the gestalt approach. The therapist knows that I-Thou experiences in which therapist and client in the depth of encounter of the moment experience each other fully are not only beautiful but also therapeutic. And I-Thou experiences do not always happen and are sometimes contraindicated.

Although the It and the Thou have been assumed thus far to be individuals, Buber makes it clear that an I may also have either kind of relationship to natural phenomena, to social entities, to the community, group, or society. Each person is seen to be in either an I-It or I-Thou relationship to these collectives or "generalized others," in Mead's (1934, 1962) terms.

The gestalt therapist shares this situational ethical stance with other philosophers, theologians, and psychologists. In addition to Fletcher and Erikson, William James (1890, 1950), John Dewey (1929, 1930), Charles W. Morris (1942, 1956), and Paul Tillich (1952) have supported these principles. In *Modes of Thought* (1938), Alfred North Whitehead asserts that one of the principal obstacles to human understanding is the simplistic notion that events can be characterized as being right or wrong.

SUMMARY

Thus far, these things have been discussed: Everything that exists is a process having as its main features change, flow, mobility, happening, and relation to other things. Everything that exists is also a part of a whole, a oneness, a totality. Knowledge itself is of two kinds—descriptive or intuitive— depending upon whether the knowing is of parts or of a whole. Knowledge itself, whether it is knowledge about an entity or simply awareness or attention to that entity, is a gestalt, an irreducible phenomenon that cannot be analyzed or explained without altering the phenomenon and creating a new one. Thus, to know is to observe and to be consciously aware of experiences in the present. The organism "knows" through its total intelligence and, in responding, it exhibits its process of "knowing."

Viewed as an integrated individual consciousness, instead of a passive register of data provided by the external world, each person constructs a personal and unique world of sensory awareness of the environment and of the structures, images, meanings, and knowledge he ascribes to at awareness. From these constructs, the person chooses personal interactions with the world, attitudes, feelings, and actions. The person also symbolizes these attitudes, feelings, and actions in words, bodily movements, images, and dreams. Both individual and environment are affirmed in the gestalt perspective, and the involved consciousness of the individual becomes the active creator of the personal experience of the world and the communicator with the world in the interaction process.

To place awareness, symbolization, and choice at the center of the gestalt model is to make a phenomenologically oriented appraisal of how life is lived, how gestalten are formed, dissolved, and reformed. And underlying this orientation, as we just noted, is an affirmation of the individual and of environmental processes as they exist, not as they are said to exist or as one might wish that they existed. Both of the latter—the beliefs about and wishes for the individual and the world—are phenomena to be dealt with. What is, is; what we do, we do. Existence, then, is whole and authentic. No aspect of living is to be avoided. All is affirmed. All may enter awareness or be the focus of attention. Each individual chooses out of the ''all'' of his experience what he will and as he will. The self is created and discovered through authentic experience.

Since all is process and everything is created or discovered interaction, two interacting processes emerge. In authentic experiencing, there is an ''I'' and there is either a ''Thou'' or an ''It.'' The aware and involved consciousness may encounter that of another as a ''Thou,'' experienced on an ''unspeakable'' level. The ''I'' may also enter into an encounter with ''It'' and treat that ''It'' as an object, as an ''other'' or external identity. Both ways of experiencing are necessary. A person's experience will flow from the ''I-It'' to the ''I-Thou'' and back.

Finally, in this process of creating and experiencing one's world, no legal or moral set of ethics and values can be superimposed upon personal experience without doing violence to the one who is experiencing. One may make a choice to live in situations accepting such a set of superimposed values; one chooses in such a case to violate personally held standards or values for the sake of something or someone with a higher priority or a stronger demand. The valid ethical stance in gestalt therapy is based upon the ethics and values of the persons who interact, and upon the situation in which the interaction takes place. Each person is responsible for him or herself in that interaction, and for the choices made in the existential moment.

Chapter 3
Psychodynamics

Gestalt therapy is a gestalt in itself—a whole that is different from the sum of its parts. In each chapter, we deal with the same whole, highlighting different parts. An example of what we mean can be experienced as you are reading this book. The book itself is the whole, including its size and shape, its cover, the kind of paper on which it is printed, the kind of printing type, and the placement of the words on the page, as well as the content of the text that is printed. As you pay attention to the book, you may focus first on the content, then on the look of the printing, then on the weight of the book, then on the content again in an on-going series of figural focuses. The whole of the book is present all the time; however, each awareness within that whole brings a new gestalt which is formed as you attend to one aspect of the whole, and then dissolves as you attend to something different. You may also change the gestalt to include yourself and your reactions as you read. In that case, the figure can be your thoughts, or the feel of the book in your hand, or an emotional reaction to the content. Each new figure brings a new gestalt that changes the whole of your experience.

In gestalt terms, the whole of gestalt therapy is the *ground,* the background or context within which we are exploring. In each chapter, we are focusing on one aspect of gestalt therapy which then is the *figure.* Thus far, we have considered as figure the psychological processes and philosophical assumptions. Now, in chapter 3 we look at psychodynamics—personality structure and personality dynamics—as figure before moving on to definitions of health and dis-ease (chapter 4), change processes and therapeutic techniques (chapter 5), and the person of the therapist (chapter 6). First, let us look at personality structure from the gestalt therapeutic perspective.

PERSONALITY STRUCTURE

Each person experiences perceptions, needs, thoughts, and emotions fluidly through a process of gestalt formation and destruction. Figure-ground relationships that emerge for the individual in experience are satisfied or resolved spontaneously, or are put aside unfinished; they then recede from prominence in the individual's flow of experiencing, and other relationships emerge into awareness. The process of developing figure-ground relationships occurs within the organism continuously in dynamic, on-going formations. Personality, then, in the gestalt therapy approach, is essentially structured out of the interaction within the individual, and the interaction between the individual and the environment. There are basic structures, and there are on-going changes.

To fit gestalt therapy into the theoretical psychological field of personality dynamics, we may say that it is related to Goldstein's (1939) organismic theory, and to the phenomenology of Lewin (1951), Rogers (1951), and Combs and Snygg (1959). The structuralism of contemporary French psychoanalysis (Lacan 1956; Mucchielle 1970), which incorporates the individual's symbol systems (particularly language) as primary factors in the individual's structuring experience, is also related. Bandler and Grinder (1975) also deal with language systems in a manner that is congruent with the gestalt therapeutic approach.

As we have noted, the functioning of the individual involves appropriate, dynamic interrelationships among the individual's experiencing of self, of others, and of the world. To understand the relationships involved in this dynamic structure, we need to look at conceptions of *organism, self,* and *ego* from the gestalt therapy viewpoint.

Organism

The organism is a totality of the essential aspects, parts, or organs functioning as a complete unit in persons. The organism, then, is the term or concept used to denote the total unit of any given person, including biological and psychological structures, functions, and processes. The organism operates according to gestalt formation and destruction principles; its primary functions are to be aware of and to regulate internal needs, and to interact with the environment to meet those needs. Out of the total phenomenal experience, the organism attends to the most compelling, urgent, interesting, or potentially satisfying aspect. Whatever an individual selects will be a product of the interaction between perceived needs (not necessarily overt and, certainly, not necessarily conscious) and perception of the offerings of the situation (Combs and Snygg 1959).

On the basic biological level of organismic responses, simple needs for such things as food, water, and shelter occur. On more complex levels, even though the process is the same, it becomes more difficult to specify in advance the particular needs of the organism.

Each most pressing unfinished situation assumes dominance and mobilizes all the available effort until the task is completed; then it becomes indifferent and loses consciousness, and the next pressing need claims attention; the need becomes pressing not deliberately but spontaneously.

Deliberateness, selection, planning are involved in completing the unfinished situation, but consciousness does not have to find the problem, rather it is identical with the problem. The spontaneous consciousness of the dominant need and its organization of the functions of contact is the psychological form of organismic self-regulation. (Perls et al. 1951, p. 274)

Here, emphasis is placed upon the closure of unfinished situations, for there is a powerful need within the organism to gain completeness and a sense of wholeness—gestalt closure or completion—in its activities. In moving toward wholeness, the organism encounters past experiences within itself that have not been resolved which cry out for resolution. These incomplete gestalten surface in the same way that biological needs surface, one at a time. The most pressing one becomes the most clear. Many times, we are prevented from dealing effectively with present situations because we are carrying unfinished past experiences, feelings, beliefs, and thoughts into the present.

One way the organism has of attempting to assimilate and resolve important unfinished situations is to bring them up over and over again. For example, you may have some unresolved conflict with your brother who is 24 years old and wears a full beard. At a party, you are introduced to a young man whose beard resembles your brother's. The sight of the beard may trigger thoughts and feelings about your brother that prevent you from either seeing the new young man clearly or listening to him attentively. This is an ineffective way of dealing with either the new or the old experiences. It may create more unfinished business in the lack of contact with the new person. When past experiences have not been resolved, they impinge upon the present; they obscure the possibility of clear, unobstructed responsiveness; they restrict movement and limit activity; they obstruct closure to which the organism is internally motivated. Enough unfinished and unclear situations can produce a truly neurotic individual.

The controls that are placed upon the organism deny its intrinsic ability to regulate itself, in addition to keeping the organism in a constantly incomplete and unfinished state. By placing inappropriate controls over the emergence and expression of organismic balance, the individual undermines this important assimilation process. While self-regulation is a natural and spontaneous activity in the organism, internalized methods of control, adopted through attempts to "adjust," may interfere with this activity.

Taught from childhood that natural impulses, natural movements, and needs are dangerous and/or animalistic, many persons learn to keep them caged or on leashes, like ferocious beasts. However, such controls are not necessarily beneficial; instead of allowing persons to move toward completion and wholeness, they often delay and deny the assimilation process. The control functions counter to genuine, authentic expression of needs. The excuse or reason for persons to control themselves is either a moral one (''shoulds'' or ''oughts'') or a fantasy concerning what might happen without careful control. Catastrophic expectations concerning consequences for spontaneous behavior inhibit the individual's free expression and open responses to situations. For whatever reasons they are instituted, such controls lead the individual to distrust himself.

A simple example of such control may help to clarify this argument. You are sitting in a committee meeting with members of a planning group who are actively engaged in a productive discussion. You become aware that you are hungry, your organism needs food. You do not interrupt the meeting, however, either to declare your hunger or to go get something to eat. You stay in the meeting and endeavor to control your attention so that hunger pangs take second place to the content of the discussion. While such control is often functional in the immediate context of a situation, habitual or characteristic control may lead to ignoring, repressing, or distorting the processes which keep the organism functioning as a complete system. Interruption of a self-regulated system requires external manipulation in order to continue the functions which have been blocked; we have to take conscious control and make deliberate decisions for otherwise free-flowing activities or awarenesses.

Self

As the organism responds to its own needs, and regulates its responses in order to meet or satisfy its needs, it makes contact with the environment. Perls (1969a) calls this "aggression" into the environment. Through these contacts or aggressions, the distinctions between the organism and the environment are sharpened. Awareness of these contact points is one aspect of the "self." In *Gestalt Therapy* (1951) Perls et al. say, "Self, the system of contacts, always integrates perceptive–proprioceptive functions, motor-muscular functions, and organic needs. It is aware and orients, aggresses and manipulates, and feels emotionally the appropriateness of environment and organism" (Pp. 373-74). The system of contacts, then, is one aspect of the self. The other primary aspect is the evaluating of appropriateness for the organism, the knowing of what is true for the organism at any moment. "The self is the contact–boundary at work; its activity is forming figures and grounds" (Perls et al. 1951, p. 235).

One way to see how the self operates is to reflect upon a time of particularly intense needs and activity, possibly great stress or heightened emotions. In such a time, persons experience contact with surroundings in sharply defined terms, and experience the evaluation of what is appropriate or true with clarity and immediacy. Let us consider an example at this point. You are driving down the street thinking about the shopping list you have decided to take care of when a car starts up from the side of the street and starts out in front of you. Immediately, the contact with that stimulus supersedes the thoughts you have been attending to, and total awareness of the environment is sharp and clear. Your "self" has organized your perceptions around the immediate need to see the situation clearly. Then comes the evaluation, in this case almost spontaneously. The need to stop short of hitting the other car leads to your jamming on your brakes and swerving out. That need arises from the ''self's'' evaluation of the event, choosing self-preservation, knowing what to do to best accomplish that, and activating the foot on the brake. These are not conscious, thoughtful decisions; they are the ''self'' in action. In many known cases, the organism responds in such immediate crisis situations with feats that seem almost superhuman. The conscious decision making processes are not involved at all. The total organismic power is available without contamination.

Take another example. You are talking intently with a friend or a colleague about a mutually engaging subject. You make a comment and, in the middle of your sentence, you stop yourself and correct your statement so that it reflects your best judgment or clearest memory about the issue being discussed. You may say something like, ''I went to Europe in 1971—no, it was in 1972.'' In this case your ''self'' has been engaged in attending to your statements and evaluating their truth or appropriateness, prompting you to change a sentence in the middle to more accurately reflect the truth. These activities of the self are internal, some related to awareness and some carried out in an unaware state. In either case, the self is related to the system of awareness in contact with the boundary between self and not–self and to the evaluation of the awarenesses and the self's responses to the contact.

The self, then, is awareness, knowing, and choice. At times, the individual may be conscious of the self system and its processes, and, at other times, the self may operate and the individual not be conscious of the processes.

Ego

Although the ego is sometimes dealt with in a pejorative manner in some psychological theory as contrasted to both the self and the organism, it is an essential part of the person in the gestalt perspective. The organism has use for the ego in mobilizing its energy and resources for the satisfaction of needs and wants. Perls (1969a) notes this as an integrative function:

The ego in a kind of administrative function will connect the actions of the *whole* organism with its foremost needs; it calls, so to speak, upon those functions of the whole organism which are necessary for the gratification of the *most urgent* need. Once the organism has identified itself with a demand, it stands as wholeheartedly behind it as it is hostile toward anything alienated. (P. 146)

Thus, the ego is an ''identification with'' or a system of ''identifications with.'' In gestalt therapy, the concept of ego is similar to the Freudian concept of the ego as a reality-oriented process. Like the self, it is not a thing but a functional experience in the organism. Gestalt therapy defines *self* as the system of contacts with the environment; *ego* is defined as identification with those contacts. In terms of figure-ground formation, the ego is the identification with the needs, desires, and experiences that are clearly figural. When a lack of something is experienced in the organism, the ego says, ''*I* am hungry,'' or ''*I* am lonely.'' Formation of gestalten (an activity of the self) and identification with the formation (an activity of the ego) are different processes. Ego activities involve abstraction of and labeling of events.

The ego aids assimilation and integration of experiences, as we have noted. In describing psychological health and disease, Perls et al. (1951) clarify ego functioning:

> If a man identifies with his forming self, does not inhibit his own creative excitement and reaching toward the coming solution; and conversely, if he alienates what is not organically his own and therefore cannot be vitally interesting, but rather disrupts the figure-background, then he is psychologically healthy, for he is exercising his best power and will do the best he can in the difficult circumstances of the world. But on the contrary, if he alienates himself and because of his false identifications tries to conquer his own spontaneity, then he creates his life dull, confused, and painful. The system of identifications and alienations we shall call the ''ego.'' (P. 235)

Ego, then, can function both positively and negatively in its effects on the organism. When the ego coincides in its functions with the needs of the total organism, spontaneous and integrated activity results. On the other hand, when the ego constructs a false identification, it closes off human experience, it categorizes and solidifies the individual's character. This negative function of ego is what is most often meant when one says that someone has a strong ego or strong ego needs: the person has a strong, unyielding identification with some particular parts of the total personality and is involved in satisfying only those needs. For example, pride, stubbornness, judging oneself or others as good or bad without evidence, admiration in the sense of exalting oneself or someone else, feeling superior, etc. are feelings and actions associated with ego needs, not self or organismic needs. Likewise, in referring to egotism and egotistical behavior, we commonly refer to over–identification with unique parts of oneself and under-identification with aspects that may be common to all people.

Identification with certain experiences and alienation from other experiences can set up ego boundaries that prevent the individual from perceiving reality fruitfully and as a source of growthful experiences. Dichotomization of experiences into right and wrong may become rigidified. Even when a person breaks down the ego boundaries, another boundary like the old one is created with the label of ''right.'' Whoever or whatever differs is automatically, then, ''wrong.''

When a person functions in such a way that organismic self-regulation completely takes over, then the ego stops functioning. The self and the organism become one, and the ego drops away. There is no need for any identification or alienation. Such functioning is related to satori experiences in the Zen tradition when one reaches a sense of unity with one's self and the world. Value judgments that exclude experiences or that differentiate experiences into categories cease to function. Such a state is very similar to Maslow's

(1962) description of B-cognition during peak experiences: noncomparing, nonevaluating, or nonjudging, embracing a holistic perception of reality.

Few persons transcend ego functioning for long. The organism needs boundaries and needs to aggress or to achieve meaningful and satisfying contact with that which is not-self. It needs to identify likenesses and recognize alien substances, things, or experiences in order to effect creation and dissolution of gestalten.

ZONES OF EXPERIENCE

We have now identified the three structures in the personality according to gestalt therapy. Now let us consider three zones of experience: interior, exterior, and intermediate, or metaexperience. The processes that occur in each zone and the interrelations among the zones determine the individual's levels of functioning and personality development.

The interior zone, which includes the organism's experiences of itself, is defined as the experience of everything that occurs within the body. This zone includes mood, emotion, proprioceptive stimuli, hunger, thirst, adrenalin surges, and so on. It does not include awareness of the quality of the experience or the process of it. While a knowledge of physiology, biology, or neurology may aid in an intellectual understanding of the range of interior experience, the individual's own experiential awareness of body states is the focus for our discussion at this point.

The exterior experience, that of the immediate environment, is gained through the senses. Awareness of the external world emerges through the individual's eyes, ears, nose, throat, and skin, and the personal associations with the phenomena that are being experienced, not through purely "objective" characteristics. Thus, the quality of peppermint candy is realized as sweetness, or texture, or a certain flavor, not as a chemical formula or a physical mass. The experience of sweetness becomes mingled with the interior experience of the body and, in fact, may become a part (usually short-lived) of the interior experience, as when a slight taste of peppermint remains in the mouth after the candy is eaten. At this point, we experience the taste as part of ourselves.

The above simplified example indicates a necessary, though often subtle, process of interrelation between exterior and interior experiences. Is this interrelation simply one of changing an exterior experience into an interior experience by receiving it in the personal framework? Not necessarily. Some exterior experiences, that is, experiences of the external environment, affect the internal processes only so long as the external phenomenon exists. An example would be the experience of the hardness of a bench. Other experiences of the environment begin a process of assimilation that continues as an internal experience for varying amounts of time after the phenomenon itself has gone, such as an event that calls forth a complex of associated emotions.

The point of transfer from exterior to interior experience varies in many ways, most of which depend upon the attitude of the person involved. An obvious example is that of chewing and swallowing food. At some point—and this is likely to vary considerably with individuals—the commingling of food and saliva turns this external substance into part of the person. Some persons may recognize this food as part of themselves even before they swallow it; others only recognize it when it is assimilated through the digestive system, an internal process that is activated by, but is not part of, the external phenomenon of food. Elimination of waste products continues this process to the final separation of the body and the waste product.

Perls calls the psychological contact between external and internal contours the DMZ, the demilitarized or middle zone of experience. Triggered by both the interior and exterior zonal experiences, it is in the service of neither. In the DMZ, thought is the controlling function, and may be realized as memory, fantasy, imagery, dreams, wishes, labels, etc. In short, it is metaexperience—experience *about* experience—that mediates, improves, destroys, biases, organizes, but profoundly influences the quality of the interior and exterior zonal experiences. The capacity in individuals for metaexperience entails the separation of cognitive functions from other experiential functions.

If you do not clearly understand the difference among the three zones, the following experiential exercise may help. As you read the following paragraph and allow yourself to follow the simple directions, you may experience each of the zones and begin to differentiate the zonal experiences.

Stop. Pay attention to what you are hearing for a few moments . . . . The sounds you hear put you in touch with the external world. They give you sense impressions . . . . Now notice any feelings you have in your stomach . . . . This puts you into contact with your internal world of experience . . . . Now think back to what you heard when you were listening. Did you put a label on it? Did you categorize the sounds in any way? If you heard a sound and thought, "That's a bird singing," or "That's a car engine," you were in your DMZ or middle zone of experience.

In the above exercise, if you allowed yourself to follow the suggested series of experiences, the only contact you had with the external phenomena (i.e., bird singing or car engine) was the sound waves hitting your eardrum. You did not see the bird, feel it, or touch it, yet you figured out that it was a bird singing; or a car engine making noise, or an air conditioner humming. What you added to the sense experience came from cognition, the middle zone. Similarly, if you felt tension or fullness in your stomach and gave it a label, a meaning, or an interpretation (i.e., "I'm feeling excited" or "I'm feeling full"), you were adding a middle zone experience to the experience of the body state.

All interpretations, labels, qualifications, images, and so forth are associated with the middle zone. Any contact through the senses with something outside the individual is experience of the outer zone, and any feelings that come from inside the individual are experiences of the inner zone. Often, we become confused by believing that how we process or think about an exterior or interior experience—our image of the experience, for example—is necessarily a part of that interior or exterior experience itself. It is not. The exterior or interior experience is an immediate and spontaneous sensation or contact. Middle zone experience is not sensation, not contact, not immediate or spontaneous. Lack of clarity in discrimination between these zones leads to confusion between experiences of fantasy and reality, which is discussed later in this chapter.

Gestalt therapy is not unique in recognizing the ways in which the individual misinterprets reality by attaching inappropriate labels to experience. Rational-emotive therapy (Ellis 1958) also concentrates upon the process through which an individual misconstrues events. According to Ellis, when a person experiences an event, that person interprets it according to his or her own belief system. Irrational beliefs about the world generate emotions within each person, but persons tend to believe that the event they experience ''causes'' their emotions, instead of recognizing that they are their own source of emotional reactions. For Ellis, therapy attempts to change a person's irrational beliefs into rational ones, for it is through such changes that a person becomes capable of developing more realistic concepts of the world and of the self. What Ellis calls ''irrational beliefs,'' Perls refers to as fantasy. Although therapeutic interventions are very different in the two systems, both gestalt therapy and rational-emotive therapy emphasize the importance of accurate, realistic perception as a prerequisite for healthy functioning of the individual.

PERSONALITY DYNAMICS

In considering the basic structure of personality, it is inevitable that we consider also the dynamics through which the structure operates and changes. Thus, we have already discussed such essential gestalt therapy constructs as organismic experiencing, identification, and alienation in earlier sections of this chapter. A more complete appraisal of psychodynamics leads us back to some of the same constructs; however, we now can take a closer look at how the personality functions as a whole.

Symbolization

Each person has as the most characteristic human endowment, the ability to symbolize all aspects of personal experience (Langer 1951; Cassirer 1946). In understanding even very simple phenomena, the individual draws upon the capacity for symbolization in diverse ways. An event may be symbolized in order to be communicated to another person, in order to be remembered by the individual, or in order to be explored mentally more fully. Mental activity in itself, whether it is engaged in abstruse theoretics or in every day manipulation of objects, *represents* phenomena. Not only does it mediate experience, it re-presents it to each person.

In the symbolizing process, mental activity transforms undifferentiated impressions into recognizable patterns, such as figure-ground arrangements, which are related by the individual to the whole of his synthesized experience. Thus, symbolization is the essence of mental life, giving the individual the ability to go beyond mere absorption of incoming impressions. The ability to symbolize allows the individual to remember past experiences, anticipate future events, establish interchanges in the present, and determine the personal meaning of them all.

In terms of personality, symbolic functions enable the individual to experience existence in a self-reflective manner. That is, on one hand, the individual is immersed in private perceptions and his views of and beliefs about the world are controlled by them. If private perceptions were the only means of responding to the environment, the individual would not be able to reflect upon actions, but would merely be reacting automatically in the way that the autonomic nervous system reacts to stimuli. On the other hand, a person is capable of construing experience in a variety of ways and is, thus, controlled more by constructions of reality than by objective events. "Man to the extent that he is able to construe his circumstances can find for himself freedom from their domination . . . man can enslave himself with his own ideas and then win his freedom again by reconstruing his life" (Kelly 1963, p.21).

Self-perception is possible because symbolization is possible. Symbolization of experience begins as a simple tool for sorting out the impressions and events that impinge upon a person, labeling of experience, for example. It becomes an elaborate process of understanding, eventually extending beyond the labeling of immediate phenomena to the describing of phenomena that are not immediately accessible to the senses. The self and the perceptual process are both displaced from immediate experience; because they can be symbolized, they become accessible to each person.

What we are suggesting is that only because the individual is capable of both perceiving and of abstracting from perceptions is the individual able to develop processes for changing experience and altering self concepts. Symbolization processes, then, are primary processes in therapeutic interventions— language, imagery, dreams, abstractions of body experience.

The ability to abstract and symbolize reality and to symbolize oneself in appropriate fashion are tied together. With the ability to abstract, the individual increases the ability to function adequately. However, the capacity to abstract appropriately is not a function of intellectual prowess but of perceptual style. Concentration upon overintellectualizing or categorizing experience tends to divorce the individual from the world-as-a-whole. For example, in a study of the experiential abilities of reluctant witnesses to crimes, Denner (1970) found that those persons most hesitant about informing store owners of observed shoplifting tended to maintain a conservative, rigid orientation toward their own experiences as well as toward external experiences. Denner found that an overintellectualized orientation toward symbolizing concrete experience leads to a conservative state in which the individual maintains a rigid overcontrol regarding interpretation of events. His subjects exhibited a similar overcontrol in problem solving situations and when asked to describe themselves in open-ended, contrary-to-fact situations.

In the healthy personality, organismic experiences are brought to conscious awareness through appropriate symbolization. Symbols enable the individual to make contact with the deepest levels of experience; their status as experiential signals leads to the organization of images and meanings within the individual. It is through the signals that the most complete experience of oneself as an independent entity emerges. As we will see in chapter 5 and in the transcript in the Appendix, the exploration of such signals is the main function of gestalt therapy techniques.

The subjective feeling of having a self and of having experiential processes that arise from within oneself are important ingredients in the healthy personality. Maslow (1971) says, for instance " . . . in most neuroses, and in many other disturbances as well, the inner signals become weak or even disappear entirely . . . and/or are not 'heard' or *cannot* be heard. At the extreme we have the experientially empty person, the zombie, the one with empty insides" (P. 33). Without the ability to hear the inner signals and to respond directly to them, the individual lacks a sense of "rightness" or congruence in the whole of experience.

This feeling of "rightness" in one's expressions and experiences has been indicated by many psychologists as an important identity experience. Erikson (1968) describes a process in which the individual is more vital and animated in daily functioning as being one in which the person overcomes some estrangement and is able to react holistically to the environment; that is, at some deep level the person "solves" a "problem" or resolves an identity dilemma. Earl Kelly (1962) says that the fully functioning personality knows no way to live except in keeping with personal values, which means that in the basic experience of oneself, in the exploring and discovering of meaning, the person has a subjective experience of valuing and of being in touch with the totality of individual identity. Horney (1945) explains that loss of spontaneity, the power to experience oneself freely, leads to alienation and emotional sickness. Maslow (1954, 1962) says that one can choose wisely for one's life only if one is capable of listening carefully to one's own needs and wishes. Rollo May (1969) suggests that, through repression of experience, modern individuals have lost their images of themselves as responsible individuals. Perls (1969b) echoes this statement when he divides the word *responsibility* into *response-ability,* suggesting the central importance of the ability to respond of each person for the individual personal experiences.

A case in point concerning the importance of symbolizing personal experience comes from the private practice of one of the authors. George, the client, was described in the following way:

He had no sense of being a real person; he felt himself to be an empty shell that functioned, but with mist and vapor inside and no solidity or strength. I perceived George to be personable, above average in intelligence, and to have an excellent command of the language. In fact, George talked a lot—about himself, about his family, about his animals, about his schooling, about his job prospects, about his girlfriends (or lack of), about his apartment, about his car troubles, and on, and on . . . and on. He talked a lot. After several sessions George confessed that he felt totally unconnected from his voice and his words, which came as off a tape recorder and floated away in space. (Korb 1974, p. 12)

George's divorce from the words he spoke highlighted the experience he had of not being in touch with himself as an experiencing, meaningful person.

Polarization

Polarization is the process through which an individual organizes and symbolizes beliefs about self or about the world. In essence, it entails establishing either-or categories or niches into which one classifies events or perceptions. Often, these classifications are made according to evaluative criteria, such as good-bad, interesting-boring, worthwhile-worthless, acceptable-unacceptable. Such classifications may polarize emotions (love-hate, sincere-insincere, etc.), perceived attributes about the self (me-not me, good child-bad child, etc.), or perceived attributes of others (friend-enemy, helping-hindering, significant-insignificant, etc.). Such designations establish boundaries that often become rigid, uncompromising, unchanging.

It is recognized in gestalt therapy that polarization of feelings, attitudes, or values enables the individual to establish definitive bases for relating to the world; it provides a simple structure for experience by reducing the complex, relativistic phenomena that a person encounters daily to discrete, predictable elements. The individual then finds it easy to interpret events and to determine appropriate responses to those events. In addition, the gestalt perspective affirms the validity of both ends of the polarization and the appropriateness of either in certain cases or situations. Both love and hate are valid emotions; both good child and bad child constructs may exist in the self-structure of the personality.

During the course of a person's life, however, more and more of experience may be reduced to dichotomous constructs, which means that more and more of experience becomes predictable and, through that predictability, lost to the individual as lived and living experience. The gestalt therapist believes that the primary motive for rigid polarizations in the individual is to maintain or establish control over aspects of the environment or of the self. By mentally pigeonholing experience, the individual uses a two-value reference system to create labels or constructs regarding life, and then proceeds to respond to the adopted labels as if those labels were, in fact, the same as the event they categorize. Control derives from the power of such labels, giving a false perspective of the range of experience. This may mean, in the long run, that people develop expectations that all things fit into neat categories and that, when they don't fit, extreme discomfort arises from the dissociation of the individual from the established categories.

On the level of self-perception, the practice of categorizing according to good or bad leads to the denial of some aspects of self and over-identification with other aspects. The symbolization of personal experience through dichotomous labels and constructs interferes with open awareness of one's own potential. Such limiting constructs are products of the DMZ or middle zone of experience—the intellect which is exercising overcontrol of the flow of human experiencing. Maslow (1962) has theorized that the two-value orientation toward self inhibits the ultimate integration of the total person:

My psychologist's way of saying the same thing is "dichotomizing means pathologizing; and pathologizing means dichotomizing." The man who thinks you can be *either* a man, all man, *or* a woman, and *nothing but* a woman, is doomed to struggle with himself, and to external estrangement from women. To the extent that he learns the facts of psychological 'bisexuality,' and becomes aware of the arbitrariness of either/or definitions and the pathogenic nature of the process of dichotomizing, to the degree that he discovers that differences can fuse and be structured with each other, and need not be exclusive and mutually antagonistic, to that extent will he be a more integrated person, able to accept and enjoy the "feminine' within himself. (Pp. 161-62)

Perls (1969b), likewise, points out the pathological nature of systematic denial of aspects of the self.

If some of our thoughts, feelings, are unacceptable to us, we want to disown them. *Me* wanting to kill you? So we disown the killing thought and say, "That's not me—that's a *compulsion,*" or we remove the killing, or we repress and become blind to that. There are many of these kinds of ways to remain intact, but always only at the cost of disowning many, many valuable parts of ourselves. (P. 11)

In gestalt therapy, both aspects of any polarization exist and are valid. The homeostatic balance in the personality may be achieved only by affirming both poles, by owning the thoughts or feelings at the pole that may have been disclaimed or disowned. Approval is not required; affirmation is required. There is, in gestalt therapy, no built-in set of approved constructs or symbols that must be accepted before a person is healthy or whole. Polarizations are present because both ends of the pole are present. In therapy, each individual discovers the homeostatic balance that is appropriate for living in a personally satisfying manner.

Contact-Withdrawal

Contact is the point where two boundaries meet. The points where the boundaries between you and me meet are our particular contacts. The points where the boundaries between the individual and the state, between the person and the person's occupation, or between two people or groups of people meet are the contacts between them. Determining the nature of contact necessitates observing the things with which a person interrelates. If someone passes by people on the street, by cars, by shop windows, by trees, and by stop lights without altering behavior in any way, that person is not interrelating with those parts of the environment. However, if this same person meets a friend during a stroll through town, stops and talks for awhile, slows the pace of walking, or in any way varies behavior because of particular events encountered, then that person is in some contact with the immediate environment.

We say that there is *some* contact, because we cannot specify the extent of that contact without further information. In the example above, in relation to the other elements of the environment, that person is in relatively more contact with the friend. However, let us suppose that their conversation is habitual, does not vary essentially from one contact to another. In terms of that habitual conversation—about the weather, family, job, for example—this person may not be "in contact" because there is no real variation in ways of responding. Our stroller may be a man who, all the time he is conversing with his friend, is thinking about an old girlfriend he is on his way to meet. In his attending to those thoughts, he is most aware of his anticipation of meeting the old girlfriend and in less contact with the friend on the street.

If boundaries do not meet, they cannot interrelate. If they do not interrelate, there is no contact. In *Gestalt Therapy* (1951), Perls et al. explain the human side of contact:

Experience occurs at the boundary between the organism and its environment, primarily the skin surface and the other organs of sensory and motor response. Experience is the function of this boundary, and psychologically what is real are the 'whole' configurations of this functioning, some meaning being achieved, some action completed. (P. 229)

The means of contact with the environment, then, are the senses: seeing, hearing, touching, tasting, smelling. One experiences the environment through them. They are the organs at the boundary between self and not-self, giving information that enables the person to distinguish and discriminate in ways that are essential for identity formation and survival.

When we say "boundary" we usually think of a boundary between. However, the contact boundary, where experience occurs, not only separates the organism and its environment, it also connects the organism and its environment, sometimes limiting and sometimes expanding the organism. The boundary may contain and protect the organism; at the same time, the organism and environment touch each other. The contact boundary can be seen and used as a way of joining as well as a way of separating. "To put it in a way that must seem odd, the contact-boundary—for example, the sensitive skin—is not so much a part of the 'organism' as *it is essentially the organ of a particular relation of the organism and the environment*" (Perls et al. 1951, p. 229).

There is no growth without contact. A plant will not grow without establishing contact with the soil for minerals and water, and the air for oxygen, carbon dioxide, heat, and energy. There is no mistaking the soil for air, the minerals for the plant itself. Contact comes out of the necessary distinction between the plant and the soil. Thus, also, in humans: contact occurs only when there is distinction; otherwise, the various aspects of person/environment would be one object, the same object. Without distinction, there is only oneness and, hence, no opportunity to make contact, to vary, to assimilate otherness, and to grow. The lack of clear definition and difference is called ''confluence'' in gestalt therapy. It will be discussed at length in the chapter on health and dis-ease.

Obviously, personal experience includes more than sensory and motor contact with the environment. As we saw earlier in this chapter, that kind of contact occurs in one of the three zones of experience. In the human organism, awareness extends into inside-the-body physiological functioning and into mental, psychological, and spiritual dimensions. In these zones ''contact'' coincides with awareness. The term ''contact'' is reserved for use in the environmental contact zone.

The polar opposite of environmental contact is withdrawal—not loss of good contact, but transference of good contact from the environment to internal processes. The rhythm of one's perceptual processes includes constant flow of contact and awareness among the three zones. That is, contact through the senses with aspects of the environment—seeing the color of the sky, hearing the sounds of trucks or a police siren, touching the rough bark of a tree or the hand of a friend, tasting the sweet-sour essence of catsup, seeing the words on the page as you read—and then withdrawal into the inner zones to awareness of a knot in your stomach, a warm glow in your chest, or a tense, tight area in the back of your neck . . . and then on to awarenesses in the middle zone (DMZ) with thoughts, memories, reflections, fantasies, planning processes, goal setting strategies, or rational step-by-step problem solving mechanisms.

We have stressed clear and distinct contact with the environment in the early discussion. However, similar clear and distinct withdrawals into the other zones are also essential for optimum functioning. This withdrawal awareness of experiences inside the skin may be of such things as opposing points of view, mixed emotions, conflicting desires or attitudes, tight or tense muscles, painful responses in any part of the body, or bodily actions or movements. Through differentiation of the separate elements in such inner experiences, a person may become aware of aspects of personal identity or self-concept. In gestalt therapy, participants are encouraged to become more aware of themselves in ways that will clarify the diffuse, perhaps confused, parts of themselves. After clear awareness has been achieved, there is a chance for assimilation and growth.

Identification – Alienation

Because of the associations that a person may have regarding any particular object or person with which contact is made, the individual tends to establish either identifications with the person or object or alienation from it. Objectively speaking, it may be possible for someone to identify strongly with all aspects of the world and, thus, to accept and appreciate whatever enters experience. However, this condition of acceptance, according to Maslow (1954) is a rarity, occurring only during "peak experiences" in a person's life. For most persons, the more common and pervasive experience is one of partial identification with and partial alienation from various persons, experiences, or characteristics of oneself. Thus, the identification and alienation processes are characteristic of the individual, and determine many of the variations in personality between persons or in one person from one time to another. Each of us identifies to varying degrees with what we are, what we think we are, what we want to be, and what we think we need to be. In identifying, we polarize experiences into good and bad, me and not-me, beneficial and detrimental. Our ego solidifies, at least momentarily. By differentiating between the acceptable and unacceptable within ourselves, we cast our lot with the portions that most support our own view of ourselves. We mobilize the acceptable and usable aspects of ourselves.

We expect from others the things which we cannot mobilize or identify within ourselves. If we do not affirm ourselves—truly find ourselves satisfactory—then we are inclined to expect others to provide the aspects that are missing. In a similar fashion, we tend to expect the external world to provide us with that which we do not provide ourselves. These expectations may not be a part of our consciousness of ourselves. However, the ego, as it identifies with or alienates itself from aspects of the environment, is functioning consciously—attending or not attending to input from outside as it chooses.

Identification with particular events, objects, or persons arises out of seeking need fulfillment through them. Perls (1969b) points out,

If you don't have your loving at your disposal, and project the love, then you want to be loved, you do all kinds of things to make yourself lovable. If you disown yourself, you always become the target, you become dependent. What a dependency if you want everybody to love you! A person doesn't mean a thing and yet suddenly you set out and want to make a good impression on this person, want them to love you. It's always the image; you want to play the concept that you are lovable, you don't love yourself and you don't hate yourself, you just live. (Pp. 33-34)

The following discussion may explain how the identification–alienation process leads from one experience or feeling into another, depending upon the individual's expectations of others.

When one's expectations are not fulfilled, when one's demands are not met, a person develops resentments. Since most people are taught that their resentments are improper, unexpressible, or impolite, they are likely to suppress them. Holding back on the expression of resentment, however, brings difficulty in communicating with others. Perls (1969b) suggests,

If you have any difficulties in communication with somebody, look for your resentments. Resentments are among the worst possible unfinished situations—unfinished gestalts. If you resent, you can neither let go nor have it out. Resentment is an emotion of central importance. The resentment is the most important expression of an impasse—of being stuck. If you feel resentment, be able to express your resentment. A resentment unexpressed often is experienced as, or changes into, feelings of guilt. Whenever you feel guilty, find out what you are resenting and express it and make your demands explicit. This alone will help a lot. (P. 49)

The stronger effect of unexpressed resentment, then, may be the feeling of guilt people may attach to it. They feel guilty about the built-up resentments, and then do to themselves (in gestalt therapy this is called retroflection) what they really want to do to someone else. They make demands upon themselves. Their guilt leads to a "should" or a "should not." "I should like him." "I should not be resentful." "I should not expect her to meet my needs." They punish themselves in this way and make themselves feel guilty instead of expressing their resentment.

Guilt itself is a demand that people be "better," or at least different, than they are, that they control their feelings and their thoughts. However, since people cannot live up to all of their self-expectations, and since people cannot live up to all of the expectations others have of them, resentments of failure are common. In every experience of guilt, there is a nucleus of resentment—a hanging on to the status quo, neither giving up the investment in the situation or person nor ventilating the anger. It is easier to identify with the guilt feelings, particularly since virtually everyone has some feelings of guilt to draw upon, than it is to identify with resentment toward someone else. Therefore, guilt becomes an acceptable, even a normal alternative to recognition of underlying resentment.

Behind the guilt and resentment lie demands that are directed toward others. These demands may also be so threatening to self-esteem that they may not be confronted directly. Failure to confront and express demands, then, leads to the build-up of resentment toward others for not living up to the often unexpressed expectations or for not anticipating those expectations. Behind such resentment toward others and alienation from them lies alienation from unacceptable characteristics within the self. Thus, there are emotional blocks based upon identification with some aspects of the self—loving, caring, or performing well, for example—and alienation from others—resentment, hostility, anger. In therapy, a person may be able to own the feelings of resentment, thus reducing the guilt, and then clarify the demands and expectations that led to the resentment. The process of immediate contact with each emotional level opens the possibility of healthy identification and eventual acceptance of personal responsibility.

Re-owning personal responsibility through identification with personal expectations makes it possible for clear demands or assertions to be made and clear responses given. If you say, "I demand that you do this for me," you are responsible for yourself; you have owned your own demands. Then the person being addressed can respond to the demand by saying whether or not he or she is willing to fulfill the demand. Both persons will know what is being said and what is being responded. Each is responsible for personal behaviors. When agreement is reached, both persons experience closure—gestalt completion. If there is disagreement, both will know where the differences lie, and these may be worked out in a guilt-free way or may be accepted as they exist. Gestalt completion occurs either way.

Besides expressing resentments and demands in order to seek solutions to conflicts, their expression often leads to appreciations both of the self and of the other person. There is almost always some residual benefit in whatever situation people find themselves, but they are sometimes so immersed in the negative aspects that they are not free to pay attention to what may be appreciated. For example, Frankl (1959, 1963) gave birth to logotherapy and its attendant philosophy in the concentration camps of Germany in World War II. For Frankl, while this experience was destructive and demeaning almost beyond belief, it gave him what he needed to develop his ideas and to increase his own self-appreciation. This position does not deny negative aspects of any situation; it merely recognizes the ability of the human organism to find beneficial aspects of almost anything—an experience that indicates the validity of the polarization hypothesis.

To review the process we have been discussing, the gestalt therapy perspective assumes that closure demands direct confrontation with and eventual acceptance of feelings of guilt, thus opening the route to recognition and acceptance of demands leading to acceptance of experiences which may have originally seemed to be absolutely unacceptable. Closure becomes a matter of how much of one's experience one identifies with and how much one alienates from oneself.

SUMMARY

In this chapter we have discussed individual psychodynamics in two ways. First, we have looked at the structural aspects of personality: the organism as a whole, the self, the ego, and the zones of awareness as they are construed in gestalt therapy. Next, we have dealt with personality dynamics; that is, with a description of the ways in which the structures of the personality operate and change, bring health and dis-ease. The major dynamic processes we have looked at are symbolization and polarization, with contact–withdrawal and identification–alienation as two essential examples of polarized processes. In the next chapter, we deal more particularly with definitions of health and dis-ease in the gestalt perspective.

Chapter 4
Health and Dis-ease

Let us begin this chapter by clarifying the spelling of one major word in the chapter title, *dis-ease* rather than *disease*. In the gestalt perspective, the process of organismic self-regulation is characterized by an innate and insuppressable need for wholeness or for the completion of gestalten. Anything that facilitates the gestalt formation-destruction–reformation process can be considered healthy. In contrast, anything that blocks, impedes, avoids, or interrupts that process is unhealthy. What is unhealthy, then, is anything that causes or contributes to discomfort or uneasiness. Discomfort, uneasiness, or *dis-ease* are signals of ill health.

Disease, in the generally accepted view, is illness for which one goes to a doctor who is expected to diagnose and prescribe remedies for cure or relief. The nature of the illness may never be understood; the doctor is the expert who can cure; the doctor controls the situation, and is responsible for the patient. In the gestalt view dis-ease is discomfort which one may not fully understand, but for which one has some responsibility. Remember that each human being is a self that is continuously interactive with the environment. Each person completes gestalten by reaching for or receiving from the environment the nutrients, either psychological or physical, that are needed for satisfaction. In reality, each person lives in an environment that does not always offer the experiences that nurture or that satisfy organismic needs, or that facilitate the completion of gestalten. Each person, then, has some responsibility not for the environment, but for the self within the environment and for the quality of the self-environment interaction.

Perls notes that societies or cultures may encourage what gestaltists label as ill health. What societies deem as acceptable ways of being and acting are seen as conforming to societal demands and values for the preservation of mores and social structures, rather than validating the inner values and valuing process. An inner validation of values may endorse some values that are socially acceptable and also may endorse some that are not. Unhealthy ways of being, then, may be encouraged by the environments in which people live.

In an unsupportive environment, each person experiences a dynamic interaction between health and dis-ease. Each has some combination of the

53

psychological qualities of insecurity, fear, self-doubt, anxiety, inertia, and feelings of inferiority, loneliness, depression, and self-pity. Each person experiences some kinds of physical instabilities at times—gastritis, colds, backaches, headaches, as well as other more virulent kinds of illness. Each person also has another set of qualities which are associated with psychological health: love, strength, confidence, courage, joy, hope, enthusiasm, trust, faith, and serenity. Each person experiences times of good physical health when all parts of the physical body seem to be fully functioning.

In the gestalt view, each person is a whole person, and health and illness states are experienced both psychologically and physiologically with interactions between those two systems. Various polarities are present in each person, creating either a balanced or unbalanced functional framework for behavior. In this chapter, we shall look more closely at the framework of values that is considered healthy in gestalt therapy, and at the ways in which health is both encouraged and prevented by both the person and the environment. In chapter 5 we shall discuss therapy as an opportunity for a client to become aware of ways in which healthy functioning is blocked; in the appendix we present a transcript of gestalt therapy in action.

HEALTH

In the course of human development, each person is taught a system of social and cultural values, primarily by experiences with parents and with school environments. Such values might be conformity or complaisance, hard work, making money, having good homes, and living in a "nice" neighborhood, revering the mother in the family, family membership itself, being an American or a black or British, or not being an American or a black or British. Many of these values, without the person's being aware, are internalized. Some of the values are consonant with the person's inner self and inner experience, and some are not. To actualize one's own inner set of values, inner wisdom, power, love, and potential—to develop one's own inner support system—is one of the goals that is central in what gestalt therapists consider as health. All other aspects of health we shall consider fit under this general statement.

Some specific values are inherent in the gestalt view of health. As people mature in a healthy way, they may be described as developing the following qualities of living, all of which are believed to be healthy. Naranjo (1970) considers such a list as a set of injunctions regarding desirable ways of experiencing. Therapeutic activities are based upon these values.

1. Live in the "now."
2. Live in the "here," in the immediate situation.
3. Accept yourselves as you are.
4. See your environment and interact with it as it is, not as you wish it to be.
5. Be honest with yourselves.

6. Express yourselves in terms of what you want, think, feel, rather than manipulate self and others through rationalizations, expectations, judgments, and distortions.
7. Experience fully the complete range of emotions, the unpleasant as well as pleasant.
8. Accept no external demands that go contrary to your best knowledge of yourself.
9. Be willing to experiment, to encounter new situations.
10. Be open to change and growth.

It should be said that such principles are not unique to gestalt therapy. Many world philosophies would include precepts such as these. It should also be noted that many cultures include value orientations that are opposite; such as, valuation of past and future rather than present, or valuation of an outside supreme authority above inner personal responsibility. It is also important to point out that this list, or any similar list such as Maslow's (1962) list of characteristics of self-actualizing persons, is not a list of "shoulds" to work toward. Rather, it is a list of values that are associated with health.

Now let us consider some of the general positive values in gestalt therapy. The ones we have selected are maturation, responsibility, self-actualization, and authenticity.

Maturation

Maturation in gestalt therapy terms is considered to be an organic, biologically intact process. For example, when a fruit is mature, it is ripe; it contains within itself the essential materials and processes to change its own physical structure, to grow as a fruit-bearing tree. A ripe peach falls to the ground; it loses its attachment to the tree, and, in contrast to its previous state, it is self-contained. However, a peach seed in a vacuum will not become a tree. It still needs nourishment, much of which is within the skin of the peach. A proper environment is necessary, for, after the pulp of the peach is consumed, the peach pit must find further nourishment, this time directly from the earth, air, sun, and water.

Perls says, "Maturing is the transcendence from environmental support to self-support" (1969b, p. 28). The peach transcends early needs for environmental support, becomes a parent tree itself, and continues its growth. Human maturation proceeds in a similar manner. The first environmental support given up is the safety and warmth of the womb at birth, then the mother's breast, then the need to have people bring food, and so on. Early stages of physical development are successive progressions of transcended environmental support. Likewise, psychological maturation necessitates surrendering dependencies upon outside support in progressive stages of transcendence.

Since persons are social beings, the process of maturation never results in complete self-sufficiency, but it does move in the direction of self-support in the sense of responsibility for the self and for its support, including asking for help when necessary. We learn to "walk on our own two feet" physically and then emotionally and psychologically, discovering that, as we let go of an external support and take that support function upon ourselves, we develop a sense of self-worth and a more effective use of our capacities for observing, learning, and understanding. Such self-support functions also include the recognition of times when outside help or support is necessary, and the capability of and willingness to request that support in nonmanipulative, direct ways.

Maturation is not easy; it often is accompanied by psychological distress. Each step in the process depends upon leaving the safety and security of a state that is familiar, even though it may be uncomfortable, and risking the tender self in unfamiliar terrain. The old and familiar defenses are no longer functional, thus, the tenderness and tentativeness in the movements into what is perceived as new and, perhaps frightening. The old and familiar supports are no longer present as they were. The parents are left at home when son or daughter goes to school. The school environmental supports are no longer present when son or daughter takes a job. The old job surroundings are gone when one takes a new job. The parental situation at home, or the school situation, or the job situation may have had uncomfortable elements, even extremely difficult ones; however, these situations were familiar and, therefore, had some measure of security.

Each step in the maturation process involves the possibility of experiencing and developing more of what is potentially possible for each person. In the gestalt view, each person has what is needed to grow, to develop, and to mature. These capacities are present but unexplored, even unknown. Each move into new experiences calls out some aspects of the person that had not been used before. Thus, each move is a self-actualizing experience—the actualizing of aspects of the person that had not been experienced previously.

Each step in the maturation process also involves an increasing awareness of the possibilities of trust in oneself to be able to handle life as it comes. A retrospective look at even very difficult life passages may include the affirmation, "I made it!" accompanied by a sense of self-worth and of trust related to how much has been learned. When the steps are experienced as too long, or the new experience is too discrepant or disjointed from the old, the person may experience acute anxiety or deep depression, or begin to behave bizarrely. The mature person will ask for help at those times.

Along with the development of the sense of self-worth and the awareness of being able to trust the self comes an increasing sense of self-identity as the person matures. In the early stages of development, the sense of identity is derived from the responses one gets from important and significant persons, who in some ways serve as a mirror in which one sees oneself and constructs an identity. This identity may be far removed from what one might really be when the authentic self is allowed to emerge and is given the nourishment it needs to grow. Maturation involves a progressive emergence of the inner self, the development of an authentic identity.

One other comment needs to be made. Maturation continues lifelong, as self-actualization continues lifelong, carrying the potential for change, for growth, for new experiences that add new knowledge and awareness. Experiences plumbed to the depths yield new possibilities for the development of self-support, self-knowledge, and trust in the self.

Maturation, then, is a concept that embraces other important gestalt therapy concepts such as these: responsibility for personal feelings, experiences, and behaviors and for the choice of appropriate responses to the environment; self-actualization, a term that denotes the process of developing more completely what is already present potentially; authenticity, where behaviors reflect the thoughts and feelings that are true to the self. We now turn to a discussion of these three concepts.

Responsibility. Being responsible for oneself means being "able to respond" to one's own expectations, desires, fantasies, and actions. It also means shedding responsibility (knowing one is not "able to respond") for the behaviors, attitudes, and feelings of others and for their expectations; but this restriction of responsibility in no way implies lack of caring about the needs of other people nor does it imply an inability to respond to their needs. When people are responsible for themselves, they know that no one else knows them and that no one else can respond to the world for them. This kind of response-ability derives from self-acceptance, acceptance of the environment as it is, and from the maturity to see both self and others in proper perspective.

Perls (1969b) believes that taking responsibility for oneself is both healthy and appropriate, as opposed to feeling obliged to do for another what one assumes is needed or desired. As he puts it:

Most people believe that responsibility means, "I put myself under obligation." But it does not. You are responsible only for yourself. I am responsible only for myself. This is what I tell a patient right away. If he wants to commit suicide, that's his business. If he wants to go crazy, that's his business . . . . I am not in this world to live up to other people's expectations, nor do I feel that the world must live up to mine. (Pp. 29-30)

Responsibility, then, also applies to internal psychological processes. Each person is responsible for thoughts, feelings, attitudes, wishes, and needs—for wanting to go crazy as well as for wanting to live and work. Since awareness of and identification with experience is essential for assimilation and for organismic growth, anything that one refuses to take responsibility for is denied attention, care, or nurturance. Just like any other growing organism, each part of the individual needs attention and affirmation, and the parts that need the most attention will hurt the most or otherwise let the person know they are in need. Each person is able to respond, and can choose to respond, to internal psychological or physiological needs.

The description of responsibility is simple, but the process of being responsible is more difficult. Many people have learned to blame others for their problems rather than to assume responsibility for their part in the problem condition. Children find it easy to say "he started it," "it was her fault," or "he hit me first." This pattern is difficult to change. "The test wasn't fair," "if only my husband were different," or "the problem is the boss, the neighbors, the children, the government. . . ." This is not to say that the boss or the government may not be creating problem situations for us. They probably are. It is to say that the gestalt perspective stresses the aspects of any situation that we create or choose to be involved in. To explore the issue of responsibility is not confession but the development of awareness of who we are and of our place in the environment. In the therapeutic encounter, a client may experiment with statements of total responsibility or obligation and, in the process, may discover what is the personal truth in the problem situation.

An implication of taking responsibility for one's own behavior and feelings is that each person is also free to choose responses in any circumstances. Gestalt therapy emphasizes this freedom of the individual, and therapists may seek ways of demonstrating to the client the personal freedom that always exists in the freedom to choose. Without a belief in such personal freedom, the individual typically becomes convinced that there is no way to change. With the awareness that each individual sets limits upon public and private behavior, chooses what is done, decides whose influence is important and whose opinions are valid comes the awareness of the ways in which each individual builds cages, sets limits, and gives away personal freedom.

When we allow someone or something outside of us to make choices that are critical for us, we give up or avoid our responsibility in a situation, and we also give up what may be essential freedom. To realize our own involvement in the process around us is difficult, but it frees us so that we know that our freedom of choice belongs to us if we want to take it. Recognizing and accepting this freedom is one of the healthy processes of growth for each person.

Self-actualization.   According to Maslow (1954), the term self-actualization was first coined by Kurt Goldstein in the late 1930s. His studies and observations of the ways in which brain-damaged subjects maintained and enhanced their organismic functioning led to his postulation that the search for ways to maintain and enhance the self is never ending. To the gestalt therapist, self-actualization becomes possible when people identify fully with themselves as growing, changing organisms. Recognition of oneself as being what one is and not what one wishes to be seems to free one from fantasies regarding perfectibility and the attendant striving for unrealistic and counter-organismic goals.

A paradox regarding the striving for perfection is that the development and pursuit of unattainable expectations actually has a limiting effect upon the individual. By identifying with fantasies that relate to conditions or qualities that *should be* or *might be,* the individual ends in what Perls (1972) calls "self-image actualization" rather than "self-actualization."

No eagle will want to be an elephant, no elephant to be an eagle. They "accept" themselves . . . they take themselves for granted. No, they don't even take themselves for granted, . . . they just are. They are what they are what they are. How absurd it would be if they, like humans, had fantasies, dissatisfactions, and self-deceptions! How absurd it would be if the elephant, tired of walking the earth, wanted to fly, eat rabbits, and lay eggs. And the eagle wanted to have the strength and thick skin of the beast. (Pp. 7-8)

Expanding upon Perls's analogy, if the eagle spent time and effort in attempting to develop thick skin, and to act like an elephant, the eagle would eventually become less of an eagle. Likewise, in persons, such a distortion of the self in an effort to become something other than what one is has serious detrimental psychological consequences. The easiest example may be the effort to take the concept of self-actualization as a program for self-development. Although the self-development effort may resound with positive possibilities, psychologically one is denying oneself, an unhealthy state at best.

Self-actualization, then, is an organismic process involving the gradual development of one's unique potential through the acceptance of what one is.

Authenticity.   In gestalt therapy, as for Rogers (1951), Maslow (1962), and Bugental (1965), authenticity is an important aspect of maturation. More than honesty or directness, although these are integral parts, authenticity refers to the habitual congruent presentation of oneself. That is, the authentic individual is open to the content (thoughts, feelings, etc.) of inner experience, and is able continuously to address the world in a manner that validly represents that inner experience. "Congruence" is a term used to designate a moment of total awareness of the equality of the inner experience, the sense of identity with it, and the overt manifestation that exactly symbolizes it—a moment in which a gestalt is completed. Authenticity, as we use the term, refers to the mature state in which such congruence is habitual.

Let us make a distinction here. Rogers and others sometimes speak of being open to one's inner experience as "following one's feelings" and are thought to support an antinomian, antisocial, anti-intellectual view: anything one "feels" is right and good; there is no need to control impulses or to consider the needs and feelings of others. Such a reading of Rogers neglects all other aspects of both his theory and practice. Such a reading is often made of the writings of Fritz Perls, also neglecting other aspects of theory and practice. Gendlin (1962) points out that Rogers assumes that "the 'feeling' one optimally 'follows' is in awareness and implicitly contains social, moral and intellectual meanings" (p. 255). By "feeling," then, Rogers means any attitudes, beliefs, values, emotions, or cognitions that are truly *felt*, truly experienced. The gestalt therapist concurs.

The distinction we make is that such "feelings" in the authentic person are self-validated and are the result of a process of self awareness and choice. Some "feelings" will coincide with societal values; some "feelings" will deviate from them; and some "feelings" will be idiosyncratic. The authentic self presents itself in harmony with experiences of both the self and the environment and with unique individual choices made with inner validation.

Authenticity is more a by-product of the maturation process than a conscious goal. The person who is free of unfinished business from the past, free of unnatural expectations of the future, in touch with present organismic processes, and in good contact with the environment will express the self authentically. No other presentation is possible. Even the choice to present oneself unnaturally will be authentic.

Now it is important to look at how the healthy processes of maturation may be blocked and undermined. We call this self-sabotaging process, dis-ease.

DIS-EASE

As action, contact, choice, and authenticity characterize health in gestalt therapy, so stasis, resistance, rigidity, and control, often with anxiety, characterize the state called "dis-ease." The term is hyphenated in this way because illness states are seen as states of psychological discomfort, states important to be recognized. They signal some imbalance, possibly some blocking of natural functioning. The discomfort may signal some prevention of the natural assimilation of input from the environment and, thus, inhibit learning and growth.

When the organism is functioning in a natural, spontaneous, dynamic way, it responds openly to internal and external events. Energy is directed toward active participation or exchange with parts of the environment with which the individual is in contact. The contact may be aggressive or passive, assimilative or rejecting, but it is appropriate for the organism and productive of states that are healthy. Blocking of this dynamic interaction inhibits the essential gestalt formation-destruction-reformation process, encouraging states that are not healthy. In the following sub-sections we shall deal with four primary ways in which dis-ease is manifested and encouraged: anxiety, leaving business unfinished, manipulation, and denial of personal experience by introjection, projection, retroflection and confluence.

Anxiety

The central ingredient in unhealthy and ineffective behavior is most often anxiety, the psychological state least tolerated by the human organism. The gestalt understanding of anxiety is both simple and profound. Perls (1969b) says, "My definition of anxiety is the gap between the now and the later. Whenever you leave the sure basis of the now and become preoccupied with the future, you experience anxiety. And if the future represents a performance, then this anxiety is nothing but stage fright" (P. 30).

In one sense, anxiety is a lack of trust in the coping ability or in the self-support system of the individual and may be experienced as "free floating'' anxiety with no appropriate, specific target. It also may be experienced as "stage fright,'' specific anxiety about or concern over objective future events. Such future events may be near (what may happen when one goes home from work) or distant (what the world will be like after a nuclear holocaust).

Fantasies about either catastrophic or anastrophic future events arouse excitement and release energy. A person may become excited in anticipation; however, often there is either no immediate appropriate outlet or the person blocks the possible actions or behaviors that are imagined; then, such imaginings generate anxiety. The energy that might go into creative action in the face of the expectations of the future goes into obsessive thinking or other mental or physical gymnastics that are unrelated to either the present experience or the scenario of the future.

A secretary may be excited about going home from work. If that excitement experience happens early in the day, she may feel anxious all day at work. If, at some point, she remembers that her estranged boyfriend may call to discuss some unfinished business between them, she may experience increased jumpiness, lack of ability to focus on her work, or a tendency to drop things. Anxiety, then, is a mental jump into the future, while the body can exist only in the present. The anxiety, however, becomes part of the present experience of the body and influences the rest of the person's responses. Since the body is not able to react to the future, it can only react to the split that occurs between the person's body and the person's fantasies or thoughts that are focused on the future. So the secretary may reach for some typing paper while her thoughts are focused on the imminent confrontation with her boyfriend. Her body does not get clear signals as to how to perform and, in reaching out, she may tip over a stack of papers.

Leaving Gestalten Incomplete

One of the main sources of discomfort for most people is what Perls calls unfinished business. For example, when one feels hurt, angry, or resentful toward another person and does not resolve those feelings in some way—expressing them or letting them go—the experience is incomplete. By holding onto unfinished experiences or avoiding closure in any way, a person invests available energy and emotional reserves in sustaining the incompleteness, leaving little energy available for encountering new situations and assimilating continuing experiences. The psychological processes are these: the dominant need for surfaces in the person's awareness; the dominant need is to complete a gestalt; the person does not do what is needed to accomplish the completion. Then, either the unfinished situation will continue to emerge into awareness as an image or a tension in some part of the body, or the person will set up some kinds of controls in order to accommodate to the sense of incompleteness. The tension may become so chronic that the person is no longer aware of it. The person rehearses mentally over and over what might have been said or done.

These controls take great amounts of energy to maintain—energy that is not, then, available for the healthy contacts in the present. A person's effectiveness in responding to new experiences and the number of new experiences that can be encountered are, thus, limited. The organism's primary motivation is toward closure; what emerges as figure, then, is business that is not completed unless the organism uses some countertherapeutic measures to control awareness or responses.

Unfinished business consists primarily of past relationships or intrapsychic conflicts that have not been resolved. Some examples of unfinished situations are unexpressed resentment or anger toward parents, siblings, lovers, and spouses; or unexpressed love, unresolved guilt, unaccepted past actions. The lack of resolution may involve other persons or aspects of oneself. When persons do not act in ways that are necessary for closure, do not forgive actions that have happened in the past, or do not accept situations as they are, healthy and energetic functioning is interfered with.

Sometimes the tension of maintaining the unfinished business is covert; that is, buried in psychological defenses that are hidden from awareness so that the nature of the tension may be masked. Sometimes the tension finds expression in the body as Ida Rolf (1977), Alexander Lowen (1967), and Wilhelm Reich (1949) have shown, through such psychosomatic complaints as ulcers, tension headaches, lower back pain, arthritis, or asthma attacks.

Psychological defenses, such as conversations in absentia may be rehearsals for the actual interactions. By rehearsing, an individual is either trying to change the past or planning expressions and reactions for the future. This kind of effort may extend as far as rehearsing a complete dialogue by imagining the other person's responses or statements. Imagining conversations constitutes one of the primary means used by the individual in an attempt to reduce anxiety related to expectations about the future. In reality, the anxiety is continued or even exacerbated by the imaginings.

This is not to minimize the possibly therapeutic nature of such rehearsals in a therapy session in which the individual deals with unfinished gestalten. (See the appendix for an example.) Such techniques will be described in the next chapter. It is to say that obsessive imaginings may be both unproductive and unhealthy. It is also to say that unfinished business buried in some kind of bodily distress is also unproductive and unhealthy. Unfinished business, thus, becomes an impediment to seeing and experiencing things as they are.

Manipulation

Discussion of healthy processes in the first section of this chapter suggests that maturity and responsibility entail the individual's ability and willingness to generate self-support rather than to be dependent upon support from others. In this context, manipulation is using one's energies to obtain and maintain support from the environment rather than generating that support from within.

If a person does not generate the necessary psychological self-support and experiences anxiety in dealing with environmental impact, that person may attempt to manipulate others into providing the support that is necessary. Manipulation, then, becomes an inappropriate, yet pervasive, strategy for satisfying perceived needs. In gestalt therapy, this strategy is believed to be a manifestation of dis-ease.

To avoid or reduce anxiety, people often develop complex manipulative behavior that may seem to them to be the only way of satisfying personal needs, but which in reality heightens their dependent behavior and separates them from healthy self-support. If an individual knows no effective way of reducing the anxiety that dominates his or her experience, any actions that seem to alleviate anxiety, even temporarily, are adopted. Individuals may manipulate themselves as well as their environments. They may pay attention to certain aspects of their own experience and ignore or avoid others. They may over-identify with certain characteristics and create rigid, uncompromising, prejudicial attitudes toward the self.

One common way of manipulating the self to stay blocked from healthy contact with the environment is the self-torture game labeled by Perls as "topdog vs. underdog." The topdog aspect of the personality is the demander-of-perfection, the manifestation of a set of introjected "shoulds" and "shouldn'ts": "I should be on time, I should keep my house clean and neat at all times, I should never talk back to my boss, I should never be angry, I should always do perfect work. . . ." The topdog, speaking only to the individual from within, is an introjection of societal, familial, or authoritarian demands. Opposed to the topdog is the underdog, the manifestation of resistance to external demands. Essentially, the underdog agrees that the topdog's demands are appropriate; however, internal sabotage assures that the demands will never be met: "I'll never be able to be on time, I'll never be able to do everything right, poor me, I'll always be neurotic." In the topdog/underdog encounter, the underdog usually wins, triggering incipient depression or anxiety.

From this perspective, it becomes easy to imagine a community dominated by a complicated web of manipulative patterns, as person after person develops manipulative styles for dealing with self or others in order to find satisfaction that is not self-generated. Such a scenario is, in fact, implied in the writings of Perls, who sees few authentically healthy members of society. In gestalt therapy, then, it is believed that, to the extent that an individual is manipulative, to that same extent an individual is neurotic.

Let us assume here that all persons are neurotic to some extent, that is, manipulative of environments for support or affirmation of feelings of self-worth. Environments rarely provide all of the other persons or the experiences, the richness and possibilities, the support and challenge that are needed to satisfy individual needs. Certainly, as Berger, Berger, and Kellner (1973) point out, Western cultural institutions have developed in the bureaucratic model in which the goal is often largely to preserve the institution, rather than to care for the needs of individual members of society. It is often necessary, then, for even healthy persons to learn how to manipulate effectively in order to survive in unsupportive environments. The distinction we make is that neurotics are unaware of their manipulations and the effect of such manipulations on themselves. Healthy persons may knowingly choose manipulative behavior when it serves them in the effort to achieve satisfactory closure experiences.

Perls (1969b) suggests that the neurotic expects from the therapist those things that are not forthcoming from the environment. In other words, in the therapeutic environment, a client will use the manipulative, dependency-oriented behavior which has been learned from the external environment. The therapist, however, refuses to provide the support that has been gained manipulatively elsewhere. When the therapist provides unnecessary support, further dependence is encouraged, thus preventing a neurotic client from reaching a level of self-support that permits the giving up of unconscious and self-defeating manipulation of others.

Denial of Personal Experience

Anxiety regarding the validity of one's own personal experience underlies the unhealthy denial of that experience. The two most common areas of concern in personal experience are feelings, especially those that are seen as socially unacceptable, and perceived attributes. In both instances, the individual discovers that some aspect of self is in conflict with the ideal self, that self which is believed to be acceptable or lovable. Since the perception of incongruity between the experienced self and the ideal self creates tension, the individual often attempts to resolve the inconsistency between the ideal self and the real self by trying to deny the existence of the offending feelings or attributes, those that do not fit into the ideal.

In traditional psychoanalytic thought, the individual is seen as possessing ego defense mechanisms that function on an unconscious level to reduce anxiety arising from unacceptable ideation or feelings. Gestalt therapy does not concentrate upon coping mechanisms in the same way; the gestalt therapist generally assumes that denial of various aspects of self operates as a general factor in handling anxiety, but makes few assumptions about unconscious drives and forces within the individual. Thus, the conceptualization of denial of personal experience is a pragmatic assumption upon which therapeutic work is based. The simpler dynamics of identification and alienation provide sufficient framework for understanding the mechanisms that a client uses to block healthy functioning.

In gestalt therapy, there are four psychological mechanisms that an individual may use to deny personal experience and to prevent healthy interaction with both self and the environment: projection, introjection, retroflection, and confluence. We shall discuss each briefly before moving on to therapeutic processes in chapter 5.

Projection. Perls (1969b) discusses projection in this way:

I suggest we start with the impossible assumption that whatever we believe we see in another person or in the world is nothing but a projection. Might be far out, but it's just unbelievable how much we project, and how blind and deaf we are to what is really going on. So, the re-owning of our senses and the understanding of projections will go hand in hand. (P. 67)

Let us look at an example so that we may have some explicit material to use in understanding projection and its interaction with sensory data. Recently, in a group discussion of personal family experiences, one of the men in the group opened his mouth to make a statement. Before any words emerged, another man said, "I know what you are going to say. Your parents were not happy in their marriage." The first man responded that he had not started to say that and, furthermore, he resented having "words put in my mouth." In the subsequent discussion, the second man acknowledged that his own parents had not been happy in their marriage as he had experienced them in the home. He had projected his own experience into the mouth of the first man. The projective mechanism, then, is that mechanism by which we attribute to other people the feelings, ideas, attitudes, and values that are ours. The second man in the example acknowledged that it was very difficult for him to accept the knowledge that his parents had not been happy together, thus also acknowledging his own dis-ease with the situation and his disowning of it through the projection.

Projection is extremely common. "You must be crazy." "You can't do that." "Johnny, what are you doing? Come here at once!" Each of these statements or questions is based on some attribution of personal feelings or experiences to other persons, or represent possible personal responses to the feelings or experiences of another person that are not owned as personal. The underlying message is "If I were you, I'd feel crazy" or "I'd be unable to do that" or "If I were Johnny, I'd probably be doing something wrong." The speaker in each case is projecting a personal world view upon someone else.

The gestalt therapy position is phenomenological: each person construes and constructs a personal life world that is unique. Each person functions in the world on the basis of observations about which ideas or fantasies are constructed. No person can know how the world is for anyone else; we can only imagine what it might be. The healthy position is to make clear observations as to what is perceived to be going on, to recognize and accept responsibility for the observations, and to be receptive to new information. Projection includes denial of important sensory information, and replaces that information with one's own ideas or fantasies.

Introjection To introject is to "swallow something whole," such as swallowing a sandwich in a plastic sack. The introjection does not "sit right" or "feel right" in the personal experience. The sandwich in a plastic bag is unassimilated; it remains as a heavy lump and gives no nourishment. Introjections are powerful impediments to assimilation because the structure of experiences taken in is preserved intact, while the organism requires their destruction and the selection of nutrients from them for digestion to occur.

Suppose some man whose opinion you value tells you that you are crazy, or hysterical, or brilliant, or exciting. You value the opinion, believe the person automatically, and do not examine your own beliefs and perceptions to see if the attribution is true, based on your experience of your self. At that point, you have ignored or denied your own personal experience and have abdicated your own discriminatory power. You may invent reasons for believing him—he is smart, he is perceptive, he is your father or your boss or your professor—but those reasons are rationalizations for bypassing your own organismic experience. The accumulation of these small "givings over" of the power of decision, perception, or personal acknowledgment to another person builds neuroses. The introjector tacitly participates in building up an erroneous identity.

We may define introjection in this way: the individual swallows input from outside without chewing and digesting it, and defines the self according to unassimilated and erroneous information. Introjection is the reverse of the projection process. Rather than placing a personal world view upon the environment, the individual accepts a fallacious world view from the environment. Either way, personal experience is denied or disowned.

Retroflection For a definition we quote Perls et al (1951):

> To retroflect means literally "to turn sharply back against." When a person retroflects behavior, he does to himself what originally he did or tried to do to other persons or objects. He stops directing various energies outward in attempts to manipulate and bring about changes in the environment that will satisfy his needs; instead, he redirects activity inward and substitutes himself in place of the environment as the target of behavior. (P. 146)

Retroflection, then, involves the redirection of energy that in healthy functioning would be directed outward into the environment for contact. The new direction is inward, as the individual does to the self what would spontaneously be done to objects or persons in the environment. The person fears what might be the outcome of the aggression—physical punishment, censure, loss of love, ostracism possibly—and does not run the risk of that outcome. In extreme chronic forms, retroflection becomes self-torture, self-martyrdom, or self-denial.

A client reports the sensation of heat or burning in an area localized under the left rib cage, although there is no physical reason for such an experience. In therapeutic work, the heat is recognized as emanating from something that seems like a bruise, the kind of bruise the client would like to inflict on a family member with whom the client is angry, but of whom the client is also afraid. The aggressive energy has become self-aggressive.

Retroflection as an adaptation of the individual to social norms has social value, for it provides the sort of control that actually does protect the individual from external threat and may, indeed, be advantageous. As Perls et al. (1951) note: "When retroflection is under aware control—that is, when a person in a current situation suppresses particular responses which, if expressed, would be to his disadvantage—no one can contest the soundness of such behavior" (P. 147).

Confluence When we are in confluence, we do not experience ourselves as distinct from our environment; we merge into the beliefs, attitudes, and feelings that surround us. We may feel safe in our confluence with our families, our jobs, or our possessions, but our own personal experience of the environment is denied. Contact with the environment is minimal. In the other nongrowth or dis-ease processes we have looked at, the boundaries between the individual and the environment are confused; the awareness of boundaries is seriously impaired with confluence.

One of the common confluent experiences occurs between parents and children. A father may have expectations of a son that are entirely out of keeping with what the son can do or wants to do. In fact, the father may not be aware of the son as a separate person; he may not experience any boundary between them. He may expect the son to be and to do just as he is and does himself. For the father, the experience is of confluence; there is no meaningful contact with the son. The son, in this case, may also experience confluence—he claims to have the same values, attitudes, and feelings as his father has. On the other hand, if the son does not take on the parental values and injunctions, the relationship will, indeed, be rocky.

In another context, confluence may have positive aspects as an essential part of what Maslow (1962) calls a "peak experience," a moment of "highest happiness and fulfillment." In peak experiences, Cognition of Being or B-cognition (in Maslow's terms) takes over; the object perceived is not seen as one figure against a background from which it is distinguished; rather, there is no awareness of anything but the object perceived, no sense of differentiation from it, no perception of it as "something to be used or something to be afraid of, or to be reacted to in some other human way." Such cognition is of Being, of wholeness. Confluence, in this context, is an intensely rich, "ego-transcending, self-forgetful, egoless" experience. Such peak experiences are momentary happenings; they cannot be planned or engineered. In the normal day-to-day reality of living in the world, the confluent experience is not "egoless" but is the unhealthy absence of necessary boundaries between the self or ego and aspects of the environment.

Since the confluent individual cannot be extricated in any way from the surroundings, the development of projection, introjection, and retroflection is likely in dealing with the world. The necessary discriminatory perceptions that distinguish what is perceived as ''self'' from what is ''not-self'' have been interfered with. Confluence, then, is the most insidious of the four inhibitors of growth we have discussed.

SUMMARY

In this chapter, we have given value-oriented definitions of health and dis-ease from the gestalt perspective. Health: to facilitate the gestalt formation-destruction-reformation process; to actualize one's own inner set of values, inner wisdom, power, love, and potential; to develop one's own inner support system; to value and to manifest actuality, awareness, wholeness, responsibility, maturation, authenticity. Dis-ease: to block, impede, avoid, or interrupt the healthy gestalt formation-destruction-reformation process with resultant anxiety and incomplete gestalten; to value stasis, resistance to change, rigidity, and neurotic control; to manipulate the environment for self-definition and support; to deny personal experience through the psychological mechanisms of projection, introjection, retroflection, and confluence, each of which encourages lack of clarity in ego boundaries and contact functions necessary for healthy interaction with the environment.

Chapter 5
Change Processes and the Course of Therapy

Given the psychological, philosophical, and psychodynamic foundations explained in the first three chapters, and the definitions of health and dis-ease in chapter 4, we may observe at the outset of this chapter that the simplest, most basic way to change and grow is through organismic self-regulation and conscious choice in a continuous interaction between the organism and the environment. Growth and change, in this case, happen in an effortless process of recognition of organismic needs—awareness of incomplete gestalten—and selection of actions that will meet the needs—complete the gestalten—and allow free movement to the next need that arises.

Consider a hypothetical woman who is at home one afternoon when a telephone call from her husband brings the message that he is bringing one of his clients home for dinner. The woman looks around the home with the awareness that it looks pretty messy. She thinks that the dinner she has planned is not very elegant, although there will be enough food for an extra person. The woman takes a deep breath, straightens the house, prepares what she has available in the best way possible, dresses herself as nicely as she can, and is prepared to meet the guest. This woman deals with emerging needs as she is aware of them, dealing with each by choosing materials and activities from what she has available, moving from housekeeping, to dinner preparation, to dressing as efficiently as possible.

Consider another woman confronted with the same situation. This woman is filled with anxiety as soon as she hears her husband's voice. Because of inner conflicts that emerge regarding this event, she is unable to think clearly or work effectively, and is not ready when the guest arrives. She ends by feeling totally distraught. She is angry at both her husband and herself, full of blame and making acrimonious charges. She has a terrible headache and upset stomach. All the gestalten are incomplete.

We could easily describe a situation in which a man would react in similar ways. Few of us are able to trust our organismic functioning, allowing ourselves to meet needs with whatever materials and actions are available, as Woman One did in our illustration. Most people have learned how not to live fully and completely, how to interfere with healthy, self-regulatory gestalt formation-destruction-reformation processes. Most people have learned how to create dis-ease in their lives. In the gestalt perspective, however, we begin with the assumption that all persons have the ingredients necessary to live, grow, and change in ways that are beneficial to them. They have learned how not to do that, how to block the self-regulatory processes, how to ignore needs, how to live with incomplete gestalten and with the anxiety, depression, or discomfort that is a consequence of such incompleteness.

Many people who behave as Woman Two did in our illustration may eventually come into therapy wanting some sort of change. They may say, "I have this problem I want to solve," or "I'm having trouble with my husband who insists on bringing guests home to dinner at the last moment," or "I'm having trouble with my boss who overloads me with work," or "I'm having a problem with my girlfriend, boyfriend, son, father, mother," or "I'm having a problem with myself."

From the gestalt point of view, such problems are a set of undesirable consequences of behaviors of oneself or of others. In the therapeutic situation, the environmental aspects of any client's "problem" cannot be dealt with unless the situation is restructured to include significant others; the focus is upon the individual; the boss, father, mother, or job is not present. The reality of the environmental conditions cannot be ascertained. However, what is present is a client with the perceptions, feelings, thoughts, memories, images, and behaviors that have been activated by the environment, and that constitute the world as the client perceives it or believes it to be. In gestalt therapy, the client is the focus of interest; what that client does with inner experiences of the external environmental conditions can be dealt with.

Our Woman Two from the Illustration may say, "I can't cope with my home life any longer. I have a constant stomachache and headaches, and I explode at the slightest provocation." The focus in therapy is that she copes by getting stomachaches and headaches and by exploding; she has learned to behave in those ways; these are her patterns of response to her home environment. She has alternatives. She may continue to behave in the customary way; she may blame her husband—if he were different everything would be fine. This may, in fact, be true. The husband, however, is not in therapy. She is. Therefore, another alternative is to look at her own behavior in an effort to understand *what* she does and *how* she does it, so that she may discover other possibilities for herself. When she understands *what* and *how,* she then has the option of making changes. She is not asked *why* she does what she does. Such reasons are usually rationalizations for behaviors and may not elicit information or insight to facilitate change. With the understanding of what she does and how she does it, she can take responsibility for her own behavior; she can choose to change her behavior and the attendant consequences will also change.

In gestalt therapy, it is assumed that there are two kinds of change: change within the person in attitudes, feelings, behaviors, demands, or expectations; and change in the environment. The therapist assumes that the client has all the tools needed to make any personal changes needed or wanted. The therapist facilitates the client's discovery of what the client is doing and how he or she is doing it, of the dynamic processes that underlie the behaviors that are a part of the presenting "problem." The therapist facilitates the client's acceptance of responsibility, not for the situation, but for the client's behavior in the situation. The therapist works with the client in choosing from possible alternative coping mechanisms, accepting responsibility for doing something to bring about environmental changes.

Within that set of seemingly simplistic statements is the gestalt perspective regarding therapy: Underlying the "problem" is a personal dynamic process—an attitude, a value, a belief, a perspective, or a psychological set—that defines the client's personal involvement in the "problem" situation. Therapeutic change must involve that underlying psychological mechanism in order to be effective. In the case of Woman Two in our earlier illustration, her underlying process might be an inner demand that she be "perfect" in all aspects of her life, or that all aspects of her life be "perfect" and, then, her own anxiety as she tries to meet this demand for perfection and, of course, fails. The nature of perfection as a desired state is not defined; it is simply unreachable.

In the rest of this chapter, we shall first look at two primary ways in which people prevent themselves from growing and changing, after which we shall deal at length with therapeutic issues that have been noted in the preceding paragraphs: what constitutes change, what happens in a therapeutic encounter, what attitudes and techniques facilitate change. In the appendix we present a transcript of one particular therapy session as an example of gestalt therapy in action, together with notations of therapeutic techniques and stages.

HOW TO PREVENT CHANGE

There are two primary ways in which we may prevent ourselves from growing and changing. They are polar opposites, as we shall see. One way is to attempt to improve ourselves, to try to change. A person decides that it is necessary to be "better" in some ways, and actively engages in reading the right books, or in jogging, or going on a diet. People devote their energies to trying first one thing and then another in order to achieve some imagined state they label as "better" or "improved." As Perls says, "Many people dedicate their lives to actualize a concept of what they should be like, rather than to actualize themselves . . . . This is again the curse of the ideal. The curse that you should not be what you are'' (1969b, p. 19). The additional trap in the self-improvement game is that most people are not only dissatisfied with what they are, but are also in continuous search outside themselves for what to become and for means to become it. They are also continuously involved in neurotic efforts to keep from exposing their imperfections.

Recall the neurotic psychodynamics we discussed as manipulations of the self: the ''topdog'' or ''perfection-oriented'' part of the person continually demanding; the person continually trying to change or improve; the ''underdog'' continually sabotaging the effort. The expectations of the topdog, having been introjected by the individual, usually are not reality oriented. They resemble abstract standards in constituting an ''ideal'' which is compared with the ''real.'' ''The real should not exist,'' says the topdog. ''Only the ideal is important. Eschew all else.'' However, it is impossible to be perfect (even if we knew what that was), yet our *shoulds* still push us toward the attainment of perfection, or ''higher states of consciousness,'' or ''self-actualization,'' or ''altruistic individualism,'' or a host of ''perfect'' states, without considering the whole organism.

Likewise, the underdog's main weapon of rationalization distorts reality by accepting the demands for perfection, believing that such a state will never be realized, and by finding reasons or excuses for failure. The topdog says, ''You should stop smoking,'' and the underdog replies, ''I know, but I've tried and I am too weak, and all my friends smoke, and I need cigarettes to settle my nerves, and . . . .'' Both topdog and underdog assume that we should change. The rationalizations balance against the demands and bypass the central knowing and choosing experience.

The second way in which one may prevent oneself from growing and changing, rather than trying to improve, is to frighten oneself with catastrophic expectations of what may happen if one really allows the authentic self to emerge, if one really allows oneself to feel, to experience, or to act in the ways that will satisfy needs, express true feelings and thoughts, or to complete gestalten. Instead of rationalizing and keeping the person stuck with trying to change, the underdog engages in scare tactics that often immobilize the person. The underdog says, ''If you really told your wife that you are too tired to visit her mother, she'd . . . . '' or ''If you really told your husband that you don't want to entertain . . . . '' or ''If you asked that person out, you'd probably be turned down . . . . '' or ''If you'd really tell your parents how angry you are, they wouldn't love you any more.'' Such scare tactics are incredibly successful with neurotic individuals, such as most of us are, who are ''unable to find and maintain the proper balance between [ourselves] and the rest of the world . . . . In neurosis the social and environmental boundary is felt as extending too far over into the individual. The neurotic is the man on whom society impinges too heavily'' (Perls 1973, p. 31).

For the neurotic, then, the present environment and the inner demands are experienced as pressing too strongly for the person to be able to react authentically; the self-structure is not strong enough to maintain itself against the pressures and demands as perceived. Two neurotic responses are available, both of which prevent growth and change and encourage dis-ease: the person may engage in self-improvement or, contrariwise, may frighten him or herself with catastrophic expectations of the future and remain almost immobilized.

Although in this discussion we have used the terms "topdog" and "underdog," in a therapeutic encounter, the client may (probably will) have different titles, names, or images for these aspects of the personality. The client's words or images would, of course, be used.

THE CHANGE PROCESS FROM A THERAPEUTIC PERSPECTIVE

The scene now shifts to the gestalt therapeutic encounter. Perls introduces the actor: "And now here comes our neurotic—tied to the past and to outmoded ways of acting, fuzzy about the present because he sees it only through a glass darkly, tortured about the future because the present is out of his hands" (Perls 1973, p. 44). What is always clear is that the client wants some kind of change. So let us first discuss what constitutes change from the gestalt perspective.

Change is paradoxical in the gestalt approach, as Arnold Beisser (1970) has pointed out: one can change only when one is truly oneself; in being totally what one is, one then, and only then, changes. Our discussion about the futility of self-improvement pointed to the change process. If a person is stuck in trying to improve and does not change, that person changes only by stopping the attempts at improvement and by allowing him or herself to be exactly what he or she is.

For a moment, let us compare the paradoxical theory of change with a famous paradox proposed by Zeno. According to Zeno, an arrow speeding on its way to a target does not move, because at any one instant of time the arrow is motionless. An instant is the eternal present, the moment of no movement; therefore, as life is a succession of instants, the arrow is motionless. Yet it still hits the target. The paradox comes from dividing time into segments so small that it gives the appearance of having stopped; yet in actuality, times does not stop, and the arrow is moving in the context of time moving.

Likewise, to be totally what one is at any time does not negate the change that occurs through time. Persons can be only what they are. When they are totally in the present, they do not have a sense of change and yet, they are changing. This seeming contradiction or paradox comes from the superimposition of two contexts, the momentary and the on-going, upon the notion of change.

Now let us look at the kind of change that is targeted in gestalt therapy. The client who comes into therapy with a "problem" experiences confusion or conflict, depression or anxiety. Although the client may experience the unpleasant feelings as an aspect of relationships with parts of the environment, the gestalt therapist assumes that the confusion or conflict are also intrapsychic—within the person. Given the phenomenological assumptions as a basis to build on, the perspective is that each person generates unique personal constructs about the world, and each person behaves according to personally held ideas about what the world and persons within it are like. Therefore, the conflicts, confusions, depression, or anxiety can be resolved by dealing with the client alone. Often the splits and confusions are not overt. The client may not recognize or acknowledge the battles that are being fought internally, but may actually be experiencing some form of battle fatigue from the intrapsychic conflicts.

The target for change is not the "problem" presented by the client. Rather, the gestalt therapist observes the client as he or she tells about the "problem" and looks for underlying processes by which the client maintains the inner state of confusion, conflict, depression, or anxiety. Gertrude Krause, a gestalt therapist and trainer, describes this therapeutic stance cogently:

All I do is attend . . . . I attempt to discover what the client is DOING. I am more interested in that than in the CONTENT of what he is telling me. "DOING" includes how he is sitting, breathing, are there any obvious tensions in his body, how he is speaking, what is the tone of his voice, his speech patterns, etc. I do not try to cover all of these points simultaneously but, as I attend, some process or processes exhibiting what he is doing become apparent. If no clues of process emerge from his presence alone, or how he expresses himself, I probably will discover what he is doing within the situation he is describing. (1977, p. 2)

Discovering the underlying process or theme related to a present problem is attempted on a verbal level by Bandler and Grinder (1975). Using a transformational grammar perspective, these authors detail the work of the therapist in discovering the "deep structure" beneath the verbal statements by facilitating the completion of sentences in the verbal presentation. For example, a client may say, "It makes me angry." The *it* in the sentence has no clear referent; we do not know what *it* may be in the client's story as it is told. The therapist helps the client to complete the sentence by adding a clear subject: "My roommate makes me angry." In working through the verbalizations the client comes at last to a personally responsible statement: "I become angry with my roommate when she uses my things without asking permission." Within the deep, i.e., unspoken, structure are the components that must be dealt with for the therapeutic change to take place.

The next aspect of the change process, from the gestalt perspective, is this: simply talking about an issue or a deep conflict or depression will not effect the completion of the gestalt that is being focused upon. Such completion comes only from experiencing, allowing oneself to feel, or to say, or to do whatever is necessary for the unfinished business to be finished. As Perls says, "Gestalt therapy is an experiential therapy, rather than a verbal or an interpretive therapy'' (Perls 1973, p. 64). The client is facilitated in clearly saying what needs to be said, not to any real person in his or her life, but to his or her image of that person. The client is facilitated in allowing the experiencing of whatever feelings, thoughts, or actions have been blocked, thus completing the gestalt in which the unexperienced feelings have been trapped. Perls notes this aspect of therapy as the ''Here and Now'' component. Krause sees it as ''the current process—what is the person DOING at this moment . . . . If [the client] is worrying about something that might happen next week, his here and now is WORRYING about the future'' (Krause, p. 3).

The last component of the gestalt therapy change process that we shall deal with here is called the ''I and Thou'' experience. The therapist participates freely and personally in the therapeutic encounter as a catalyst, frustrator, or clarifier, not as a familial support. A goal in gestalt therapy is to increase the client's self-support system. Therefore, any advice giving or problem solving is counterproductive; it may ''weaken a person's self support . . . anything I do to increase [my clients'] leaning propensities is the opposite of what I really wish to do—help them become more self-supportive'' (Krause, p. 3). Perls states that,

. . . if the environmental support the patient expects from us is not forthcoming, if we don't give him the answers he thinks he has to have, if we don't appreciate his good intentions, admire his psychological knowledge, congratulate him on his progress, we shall get the negative cathexis of frustration. But gestalt therapy also constantly gives him much of what he wants—attention, exclusive attention—and we don't blame him for his resistances. In this way therapy starts out with a certain balance of frustration and satisfaction. (Perls 1973, pp. 50-51)

Focal words in the preceding paragraph are these: ''we don't blame him.'' The gestalt therapist communicates radical respect for every aspect of the client—the topdog, the underdog, the pattern of resistances. The therapist assumes the ability of the client to generate self-support, and communicates that assumption and belief by a lack of familial support. The skill of the therapist is indicated by the way in which the frustration of the client is balanced with the way the therapist attends to the client and the respect that is communicated.

STEPS IN THE THERAPEUTIC PROCESS

Expression

The first step in any therapy, including gestalt therapy, is to express overtly, in some fashion, what the inner experience is so that an objective look at the experience is possible. In our earlier discussions, we considered some aspects of the assumption that each person is a dynamic whole, even though the psychological experience may be fragmented. We considered that each person, being whole, would portray personal experience in every aspect of being—words, tone of voice, images, body movements, muscles, and organs of the body. These aspects of the person will all signal the inner experience in some way. The therapist will observe such signals as a foot tapping, or a harsh tightness in the voice quality, or shallow breathing, and will facilitate the client's awareness of these overt manifestations of possible distress. The therapist suggests; the client knows or can discover the meaning of his or her experience.

For example, a male client recounts an incident that happened with his wife. As he talks, his voice is fairly steady, his posture is erect, his feet are crossed, and his hands rest on the arms of his chair. He relates the incident slowly and then at one point, although nothing changes in his voice or his posture, his right foot begins to move up and down in a fashion that is discrepant with the rest of his self presentation. His foot is signaling some inner process that is not being considered overtly. The therapist may decide to suggest some experimentation that can bring out what the foot is signaling, and the client may agree to take a look at whatever inner phenomenon the active foot signals. Only when the inner experience is brought out overtly can any therapeutic interaction take place.

Differentiation

Because the roots of conflict, confusion, depression, or anxiety lie in the processes used to prevent the client from full and complete experience, one of the assumptions that can be made is that an inner battle is probably going on. The male client may have some kind of battle between the aspect of himself that recounts the "problem" and the aspect that is represented in his foot motion. A person releases conflicting sides by differentiating between them. Through awareness, the processes in which one is engaged are recognized. The interaction between conflicting parts is the most important thing to recognize, but it remains hidden unless the conflicting factions or aspects are separated. The second stage in the therapeutic process, then, is differentiation.

The goal of the differentiation stage is to facilitate the client in recognizing the alienated, disowned, or fragmentary selves within. Here, the primary tool of the therapist is experimentation: suggesting activities through which the client may arrive at clarity as to the aspects of the inner experience that are confused or in conflict. In the case of the male client described above, the therapist may suggest the personalizing of the energy that keeps his foot moving. The therapist may simply call attention to the foot motion and suggest that the client move the foot faster or more intensely—exaggerate the motion. The therapist might suggest that the foot could be seen as having a life of its own and its own voice. At this stage, the interventions are made in an effort to concretize the client's experiences in order to help the client to be aware of himself. The kinds of interventions come from the therapist's own awarenesses, learnings, thoughts, ideas, the therapist's own creative juices. Zinker (1977) notes these characteristics of the creative therapist:

- a good sense of timing;
- the capacity to detect where the person can be reached, energized, moved emotionally;
- a knowledge of where the psychological "buttons" are and when to push them;
- the ability to shift gears—to let go of some things and move on to other, more lively areas;
- the willingness to push, confront, cajole, persuade, energize the person to get the work done;
- and the wisdom to know when to let the person stay confused so that he may learn to evolve his own clarity. (Pp. 57-58)

So, our male client may become aware that in his foot movement he is expressing frustration with the relationship with his wife, or with his wife's actions, frustration that was not being expressed in his voice, words, or other body movements. The frustration probably has been suppressed; his allowing it to surface only in his foot and without conscious awareness would indicate that it has been given little attention. And with this awareness of frustration, he has the opportunity to differentiate that feeling from the thoughts or behaviors that are manifest in his words and tone. Perls (1973) uses the term "discrimination" for this aspect of therapy: "In therapy, then, we have to re-establish the neurotic's capacity to discriminate. We have to help him to rediscover what is himself and what is not himself; what fulfills him and what thwarts him. We have to guide him towards integration. We have to assist him in finding the proper balance and boundary between himself and the rest of the world" (p. 43).

Affirmation

The next stage, then, follows immediately: the therapist will encourage the client to own the differentiated parts. Some therapists use the term "acceptance" here: the client is encouraged to accept all of the parts that are emerging into awareness. Some therapists use the term "affirmation" or "identification with." Whatever the term, at this stage the client is encouraged to invest himself in the experiences, not that he necessarily likes what is emerging but that he acknowledges each part as himself. "I am my foot—I am frustrated," and "I am my voice and I am controlling myself in order to prevent my parents from knowing that I am having marital problems," for example. Both statements may be true, even though conflicting.

A friend of ours recounts a time in her life in which she was going through a lot of changes and was uncertain about her goals. In order to keep focused upon how she felt at any one time, and to convince herself that it was all right with her to be in flux, she devised a verbal formula. In it she would make a statement about what she was aware of doing—even the most simple tasks or the most awful feelings—and then say, "and that's okay." She did not always feel okay, but the simple verbal acknowledgment continually discriminated the okay part from the not-okay part and encouraged an objectivity and an affirmation that, no matter what the content of the awareness, she was truly doing it. This general acknowledgment of herself was the start toward determining what she really wanted and toward the clarity and strength to choose for herself.

An important inhibitor or acceptance or acknowledgment of oneself is the belief that a person must be consistent, uncontradictory. The need for consistency, however, is often tied closely to the demand for perfection. In reality, each person can and does contain contradictions, paradoxes, and inconsistencies. Complexity and changeableness may be central ingredients in the gestalt formation-destruction-reformation processes.

With the acknowledgment of the conflicting or warring elements inside, the client may see a life pattern emerging that has been hidden from him in the confusion he experienced or in the "problem" that he was trying to deal with. Our male client may become aware that he has spent most of his life pretending to his parents that his life is going along smoothly in order to keep a good image with them, or in order to keep their love and attention. Such life patterns are common. Or he may discover that he is also controlling himself so that his wife will maintain a good image of him, as he sees it. He may discover a six-year-old child within who never felt accepted. Or any of a myriad of other patterns might emerge from the seemingly simple experiment of moving his foot and becoming aware of its meaning for him.

One further aspect of the affirmation stage is very important. With awareness and affirmation of the experiential phenomenon also comes awareness and affirmation of responsibility for whatever aspects of the phenomenon come within the personal, individual sphere. Our male client may say, "I am my foot, I am frustrated. And I am responsible for my frustration. I am not responsible for my wife's behavior that triggered it. I am responsible for my own reactions to her behavior." Or, "I am responsible for living my life in order to gain my parents' approval. I am not responsible for them and their demands on me. I am responsible for my perception of their demands and for what I have done and am doing in response to their demands as I perceived them." As Perls says, "Responsibility is really response-ability, the ability to choose one's reactions" (1973, p.79). The neurotic having "abdicated responsibility . . . has also given up his response-ability and his freedom of choice." Part of the work of the therapist is to help the client be clear as to what aspects of his experience he is willing to take responsibility for, and to be aware of where the limits of personal responsibility are set.

Choice and Integration

Affirmation of personal awarenesses and responsibilities brings a new stage in therapy with two new psychological possibilities: choice and integration. When the above client becomes clear about his differing parts and owns them both, he is, then, in a position to choose behaviors that fit either one or both. He may choose to confront his wife with his frustration, or he may choose to be honest with his parents as to his conflicting feelings, or he may make any of several other possible choices. Made with awareness and affirmation, any of these choices may be right for the client at that time.

The client's "problem" may be resolved through the choices made. The goal for the therapist, however, is the educated awareness of the client as to what the client is doing, how it is being done, and any life patterns that may emerge from these awarenesses. Conscious awareness facilitates choice by enabling the individual to be what he or she is, without trying to be what he or she is not.

On the preconscious level, when the conflicting energies are differentiated and owned, an internal integration often takes place that releases tension and brings calmness. This calmness is often a signal of a completed gestalt, the sense of satisfaction that comes when a situation is finished. Perls says, "The prerequisite for full satisfaction is the patient's sense of identification with all the actions he participates in, including his self-interruptions. A situation can only be finished—which means full satisfaction can only be achieved—if the patient is totally involved in it" (1973, p. 111).

In the therapy session transcribed in the appendix, the stages in the therapeutic process and the sense of calmness and satisfaction at closure, at least for that session, are noted.

THERAPEUTIC TECHNIQUES

Gestalt therapy is pursued in two settings—one-to-one work between client and therapist in an office or other work space, and one-to-one work between client and therapist in groups. We shall first look at some of the therapeutic techniques used in one-to-one work, and then make some comments about the uses of both individual and group settings for therapy. The comments about technique will be general; several statements of games and specific techniques are available, notably Levitsky and Perls 1970; Yontef 1971; Greenwald 1972; Pfeiffer and Pfeiffer 1975; and Hatcher and Himelstein 1976, Part III.

When a therapist depends upon techniques as working tools, the coherence of the gestalt approach will be missed. The therapist has little choice in the therapeutic situation, going with the design of the technique rather than with the client's experience. A therapist who follows a set of techniques is functioning in a closed system (ideas and thoughts) as opposed to an open system (organismic responses); for example, it is known that there is a pattern in many persons that relates guilt, resentment, demands, forgiveness, and gratefulness. In therapy situations, the therapist may direct a client to express guilt as resentment, turn resentment into explicit demands, and then allow whatever forgiveness and gratefulness is experienced to be expressed. However, this pattern is not always present. A client may affirm guilt feelings and experience closure at that point, so far as the immediate work is concerned. In pushing the client to fulfill the pattern by going on to resentment and demands, the therapist is relying upon a set formula. The therapist who functions in an open system knows the formulas and is willing to abandon any structures in favor of observations of the moment-to-moment signals the client is giving about the ongoing experience. Creative experimentation is called for.

In this section we shall look at some of the formulas. However, let us first review some of the beliefs and assumptions upon which such therapeutic tools are based. Recall the assumption of wholeness that is central in the gestalt therapy orientation. That is, each person is a whole organism, whether or not that wholeness is experienced. Personal experiences, of which the client may be unaware, are signaled in every aspect of the person—bodily feelings and movements, voice, tone, words, postures, images, even dreams. The gestalt therapist, in designing experiments to suggest to a client, may choose an intervention that focuses on any observed aspects of the client's presentation of him/herself. What is figural for the therapist may be a foot moving, a quality in the sound of the voice, the breathing process, or a pattern in the verbal expression. As the client speaks, the therapist may become aware that an image is forming based upon what the client says, and may suggest using such images in the therapeutic experimentation.

Let us also recall the phenomenological base in gestalt therapy: each person construes the world uniquely; each person is the sole arbiter of the world in which he/she lives. How the world is construed is described by Merleau-Ponty (1964), that is, there are *levels of experience*. The primary reality is the perceived life-world, the world that is constituted by the immediate, concrete, subjective experiences of the unique individual. It is the world of familiar, natural environmental components—both objects and persons. That world is one level of reality or experience. Other levels are of the imaginary, ideality, language, culture, and history (Edie 1964). In gestalt terms, the primary level is the immediacy of perception, sensory data, bodily experience, and feelings. These data are constituted into an experience of a life-world by the ongoing conscious awareness of the person in ways that are unique. And other levels of experience are equally important; these are activities of the mind— imagination and memory. Therapeutic techniques that start with mental activity (such as remembered events, fantasies of the future, or images of any kind) must be brought into an immediacy for therapy to be successful.

Our considerations of psychodynamics are important here, particularly polarization. The individual establishes either-or categories or classifications that provide simple structures for reducing the complex relativistic phenomena that a person encounters daily to discrete, predictable elements. A daughter either loves or hates her parents; a book that has been read has provided either a significant or an insignificant experience. The gestalt therapist assumes the existence of such polarities. If a client reports experiences of deep depression, the therapist assumes the possibility of, or perhaps an earlier experience of, great joy. The therapeutic work often consists of experiments through which both poles of the client's experience are brought into awareness and affirmed, thus releasing the client to an ongoing perceptual, thinking, feeling, organismic flow of experience or to the choice of actions and behaviors that seem appropriate. Both poles of any inner experience are affirmed, as well as the client's right to choose responses in any situation that is brought to the therapeutic encounter.

One experiential ingredient must be considered. The goals of therapy are two-fold: awareness and achnowledgment of personal experience regardless of content and, issuing from that, the development of the self-support system of the client through conscious and responsible choices. The first goal, the awareness and acknowledgment of personal experience, is the central ingredient in the completion of gestalten that have been incomplete heretofore. The male client with the tapping foot has incomplete gestalten regarding his wife or his parents or perhaps both. Awareness of what has been repressed or avoided may lead to the sense of closure that the organism is striving for.

The gestalt therapist believes that closure comes with the experience of *personal congruence* (Rogers 1959; Gendlin 1962). Carl Rogers defines personal congruence as the state in which "the self as perceived equals the actual experience of the organism, accurately symbolized" (1959, p. 206). In this statement, we note three parts of the congruent experience: the self as perceived, the actual experience of the organism, and the accurate symbolization of the actual experience. When all three are equal, a congruence is experienced.

When our male client is aware of tapping his foot, of feelings of frustration associated with the tapping, and he says, "I am frustrated about my wife's conduct," with just the right intonation and intensity, he acknowledges the whole of his experience to be a part of his self-structure. At that moment, he experiences congruence, wherein the "felt meaning" is experienced as truly represented in the words being spoken (Gendlin 1967). The personal meaning, beyond the mere words employed, is affirmed with a sense of inner relief. At that moment, the gestalt regarding our client's frustration is completed, a previously disowned or unaware aspect of himself is integrated, and he is free to experience the next gestalt, whatever his organism brings to his awareness in the next moment.

Sometimes the client will present clear data for experimentation. However, more often, the client is experimenting with material that is new and heretofore unsuspected. The experience in this case is fraught with the risk of leaving the known and moving out into uncharted territory. Psychologically, such movement requires that some self-support be present and that the client trust the therapist to an exceptional degree. The client may balk—express resistance to the experiment being suggested, or avoid dealing with something the therapist says or suggests. Then the resistance becomes a psychological entity to be dealt with through experimentation. Many therapists feel that the whole of a therapeutic interaction might be characterized as dealing with resistance. Some therapists confront resistance head-on; others deal more gently, letting the client move slowly, and giving the client no antagonist, no one to resist. Such therapeutic choices fall within the style and beliefs of individual therapists.

One important set of therapeutic techniques to single out for emphasis are those that deal with verbal communication. Often, a client may be threatened by abrupt movement into imagery or body experience; such personal experiences may have been cut off from awareness since childhood. Verbal communication is often the primary representational device and, although it is the most subject to distortion or confusion, it is the least threatening to a client. Bandler and Grinder (1975) have suggested that what has seemed like "magic" in the therapeutic work of Perls, Virginia Satir, Milton Erickson and other "charismatic superstars" is in large part related to the way in which these therapists see through the structures of the language being used to the metalevel processes that underlie it. The pain, frustration, and confusion of the client lie there. Such seeming "magical" therapeutic work can be understood by studying the linguistic bases of the language; learning the primary ways in which the language may distort, delete or generalize the experience; and designing experiments through which the deep structure of the language may emerge so that underlying meanings and feelings may surface.

Another powerful therapeutic medium in gestalt therapy is imagery or dreams. Both media involve the emergence of the contents of the preconscious, that part of the psychological experience that is not in the conscious awareness but is available to awareness. Imagery is active while the conscious rational thought processes are interrupted; dreams emerge while they are dormant. In gestalt therapy, both are considered to be avenues through which unfinished gestalten emerge into awareness. Although the symbolic "language" is metaphoric—that is, any image may mean anything and usually does signal meanings that are far removed from the nominal content—it is rich in therapeutic possibilities.

In choosing to intervene in one aspect of the client's experience, such as the imagery, the therapist keeps efficiency and effectiveness in mind. Immediacy experiences are simple rather than complex in idea, and deep rather than superficial in emotional content. Often, the therapist prefers to explore nonverbal rather than verbal avenues. The use of art materials in therapy is often advantageous. The sketch of an image using crayons and newsprint may expedite awareness and lead to experiences of great depth and intensity. Interventions using body awareness may also be helpful in a client's work in difficult and threatening areas of experience. The client's awareness of and consent to what is being done is critical.

Since images, fantasies, or dreams are seen as metaphoric expressions of content of the self-experience, a therapist may use techniques that will raise recessed material to a conscious level. The client's willingness to interrupt the conscious controls customarily placed upon imagined material, or the willingness to interact with content from a dream that may seem bizarre or unusual will release preconscious material into recognizable structures and patterns. The medium is bringing a message to the client. Perls (1969b) says, "I believe that in a dream we have a clear existential message of what's missing in our lives, what we avoid doing and living and we have plenty of material to re-assimilate and re-own the alienated parts of ourselves" (p. 76).

First person experiences are the most powerful because they sustain direct contact with the events that are being dealt with. Contact with disowned or disliked aspects of the self is difficult to maintain. Clients may say, "You know how you feel when you think about a bad experience," instead of what may really express the first person experience—"I feel very sad." Staying with the "I" of experience is rewarding and demanding, especially in dream or imagery work in which the metalevel content may be intense and powerful. Each aspect of a dream may be seen as a projection of some facet of the client or of the world of the client's experience.

Whether the therapeutic medium is body language, imagery, verbalization, or dream, an essential ingredient in the therapy is what may be called "acting." The client is encouraged to allow him or herself to *be* and to *act for* the attributes, actions, feelings, or persons that are involved in the polarities being focused upon. Naranjo (1976) points out that the acting out of polarities within the individual serves to implement expression by transferring experience from one expressive modality to another; that is, to give motoric expression to an idea or image. Thus, by avoiding the usual verbalizations as means of exploring personal experience the individual heightens involvement in the therapy in physical, nonverbal fashion.

Thus far, we have dealt with some generalizations about therapeutic techniques. There are, however, what Pfeiffer and Pfeiffer (1975) note as "classic experiments"; that is, techniques that have been used with good results, some of which have become a part of the general skill package. From our previous discussion, the techniques may now be seen as efforts to arrive at both clarity and at the psychological closure state of owning or claiming what is clearly experienced.

Dialogue: This technique is known colloquially as the "empty chair" experiment, and it is probably the best known and most often adopted by therapists of other orientations. It is a primary tool for achieving clarity. Whatever aspect of the client's world is not clear is separated from the client psychologically by the device of imagining it in a chair or some other place where the client can address it. Giving voice to the thoughts and feelings of both the client and the unclear part in a dialogue can bring insight and clarity. Both poles of an experienced phenomenon can be explored.

Exaggeration: In dealing with confusion, particularly where feelings are involved, it is often appropriate for the therapist to suggest that the client exaggerate some motion or some speech pattern. Feelings that have not been dealt with may not surface clearly until such an experiment is tried. The client may not be aware of the truth of a statement until exaggeration brings the inner experience into focus.

Reversal: Polarities are always present, and the reversal technique usually brings out the existence of both poles. Hate and love may both be present; needs to reach out and to pull back often exist simultaneously. To suggest that a client reverse a statement as an experiment often is useful in awakening awareness of essential ingredients in effecting closure.

Rehearsal: In arriving at clarity out of confusion, a client may need to try out or rehearse different sentences. Sometimes a client becomes aware of the truth of personal experience only in the act of speech. At the impasse in therapeutic work, when the client has reached the limit of environmental support but the self-support system is not yet strong, he/she may have catastrophic expectations regarding any change. Explicitly stating these fears and expectations often helps in dealing with the imagined catastrophies by adding a reality contact that was missing.

Making the Rounds: In working with a client to discover some personal truth, a therapist may suggest an experiment for a client to rehearse with each member of the group present at the time. The contact with the individual group members brings a human environmental dimension that often helps the client to be clear.

Exposing the Obvious: Perls had one dictum for therapists: pay attention to the obvious. The deep structures and processes are often revealed in a client's first statements or obvious body movements. Techniques to expose the obvious are usually reports of observations of what the client is doing. "Are you aware of any sensation in your jaw?" is an example of such an observation a therapist might make when noticing some tightness in the jaw muscles.

Directed Awareness Experiments: Contact is an essential ingredient in the therapeutic process—contact with both the personal inner experience and with the experience of the outside world. Clear seeing, hearing, and touching, as well as clear sensations in the body are the bases for contact. A therapist often designs experiments to enable a client to be aware of ways in which the sensory data may be either contaminated or ignored.

One issue remains for discussion in this section on techniques. The therapeutic work of the client is experiential, as we have said, and experience happens at what, in gestalt therapy, is called the ego boundary or contact boundary—the border between what the person experiences as "me" and known, and what is experienced as "not me" and unfamiliar. Through clear contacts with the environment, the person is nourished and excited. With unclear contacts, the person may be deadened, bored, or stultified. Contact is always immediate, always experimental, always risky. Furthermore, contact occurs when the entities within and without the boundary are clearly differentiated. Personal contacts occur at what the Polsters call the ''I-boundary'' (Polster and Polster 1973). The I-boundary, or ego-boundary, is made up of many contact points or contact areas, such as contact with other persons, with thought processes (ideas, images, memories, and so forth), with actions, with values or beliefs, with things in the environment. In each engagement there are two aspects: the primary contact with the world outside and the reflection or resonance within the self that is stirred by the contact. The resonance includes a knowledge of whether the contact initiates an experience which is welcome or one which is too risky to contemplate or to act upon. The I-boundary, then, represents the limit of what the person permits the self to contact meaningfully.

When a healthy person is engaging in permissible contacts, there is ease and excitement. In the neurotic person, permissible contacts may be controlled to the point of boredom or deadness. A therapist suggests experiments with a client in order to discover the contact boundaries in whatever psychological configuration is being focused upon. Lore Perls, an eminent therapist, notes that ''experience is on the boundary . . . . If you go too quickly beyond the boundary you may feel unsupported, actually, that's what I work with: a concept and experience of contact and support. Certain supports are necessary and essential. Other supports are, well, desirable and possibly usable. The lack of essential support always results in anxiety'' (L. Perls 1978, p. 25).

There is no royal road to therapeutic change; there are probably as many avenues to successful therapy as there are therapists to choose them. Choices of interventions are matters of creativity, training, and experience. The art and skill of the gestalt therapist is engaged in designing experiments or using classic ones that will move the client to the contact boundary, clarify the boundary functions (seeing, hearing, touching, feeling), and mobilize the self-support for meaningful, clear, and authentic contacts that are both nourishing and exciting. Other important criteria are ease, efficiency, and effectiveness, as well as personal preference. All of this must be accomplished while communicating radical respect for whatever the client presents.

Now that you have read both the sections on stages in the therapeutic process and techniques in therapy, you may wish to turn to the appendix and study the transcript of a session which illustrates their appearance as a therapist works with a client. You will find notes on both the stages and the techniques and attitudes of the therapist.

INDIVIDUAL AND GROUP WORK

Gestalt therapists work in two settings: one-to-one interaction between client and therapist in a private office, and one-to-one interactions within a group setting. Many therapists work in both ways; some prefer one setting over the other. Late in life, Perls is quoted as saying that individual therapy was obsolete (L. Perls, 1978, p. 22). In the last five years of his life, he was primarily leading demonstration workshops and using the "hot seat" method. His wife Lore, however, reports that she believes such a stance is limiting and, perhaps, even ineffective, particularly with clients who are not functioning effectively (p. 23). The choice of setting, then, is a personal preference of a particular therapist, as is the choice of therapeutic interventions.

An interesting aspect of the group experience is that, although the group members are present, the therapeutic encounter is between a client and the therapist. The group becomes a Greek chorus or a sounding board and, as structured by the therapist, may not be involved at all in the therapy or may be very much involved (Korb and Themis, 1980). The therapist is a directive leader and orchestrates all aspects of the therapeutic interactions, with the advice and consent of the client who is working. The group offers support and is available for rehearsal of important contact functions that the client may be working on.

One important aspect of the group process is the effect of work on other group members who may be stimulated to do their own work silently or to awareness of work that needs to be done with the therapist's aid. Because the therapist takes a directive leadership role, the experience of the group members is often intense and personally very satisfying.

SUMMARY

We have seen that, according to gestalt therapists, growth and change are common to the human condition, and that persons are considered to have within themselves all of the ingredients and tools for living in healthy, satisfying, immediate interaction with their environments. Dis-ease results when such healthy possibilities are blocked, interrupted, or interfered with. Change processes, then, are always present, and therapeutic change processes are those that confront the blocks and interruptions, that bring clients to immediate awareness of what is being done, said, thought, or felt. Change comes with being aware of what one is, not by trying to be what one is not. The course of a therapeutic interaction involves these steps: bringing out in some fashion what is being experienced within, differentiating or discriminating among all of the aspects of that experience, affirming or accepting the fact that all of these are, indeed, aspects of the self whether approved of or not, awareness of behavioral choices that are available, and the psychological integration that comes with the affirmation of previously disowned or unaware aspects of experience.

Many therapeutic techniques may be used by gestalt therapists; the importance of such techniques is that they be experienced, not just talked about. The therapist's art and skill are engaged in suggesting experiments that enable clients to discover and to permit contact with the boundary between what clients are aware of and will allow into awareness and what is new to them and, therefore, risky to deal with; and, then, to be totally present as clients move into healthier and riskier ways of interacting with both self and the environment.

Chapter 6
The Therapist, Person and Role

All therapies carry with them explicit and implicit standards regarding the role that the therapist engages in with clients. Such role expectations are derived from the experience and practice of therapists throughout the last century, regardless of their theoretical orientation, and also from the formal theory of health, adjustment, and change espoused by the particular therapies themselves. Thus, while there may be some significant technical or theoretical differences among therapies, they share many common concerns and expectations. In fact, a famous study of Fiedler (1950) indicates that experienced therapists of whatever original, theoretical orientation share more concepts of appropriate therapeutic relationships with each other than do experienced and inexperienced therapists of the same theoretical orientation. This finding has led many therapists and researchers to conclude that the quality of the therapeutic relationship is of more lasting importance than the particular framework or orientation in which the therapist is trained.

Even though common threads may be woven throughout the major therapies, gestalt therapy is sufficiently different to warrant a close look at the therapist as a person and as a professional, and at the particulars of the client-therapist relationship from this orientation. In this chapter we shall draw upon the material discussed in chapter 5, dealing with it from the perspective of the therapist.

PERSONAL QUALITIES

In previous chapters, we have indicated the ways in which a balanced or integrated organism responds to its environment. We described awareness of organismic processes and openness to their expression or fulfillment as being a natural aspect of being human. We outlined the dynamics of gestalt formation-destruction-reformation, the dynamics of growth and change in the organism, and the integrating process in each person. The competent gestalt therapist, a trained professional, has reached a high level of personal awareness and ability to maintain awareness of personal processes. This does not mean that the therapist always functions as a model human being, but it does mean that the therapist provides additional facilitation of growth and change in the client through being an appropriate model of the healthy processes promoted in gestalt therapy.

The therapist's own awareness, the assimilated skills and knowledge of theory and dynamics, and his or her personal characteristics are integrated. The therapist is able to trust the organismic flow of experience during the therapy session because the therapist is aware of and deals directly with needs and desires. Instead of denying intuitive private experience in favor of clinical analysis, the therapist integrates the two while working with the client. In short, the therapist is authentic, whole, and genuine, just as the client is encouraged to be.

Authentic behavior in the therapist is important in several ways. When the therapist is authentic, the possibility of building trust with the client increases dramatically. Spontaneous, flowing responses to new situations on the part of the therapist heighten the interaction between therapist and client. The willingness to be authentically oneself and the willingness to express oneself fully in the role as therapist or group leader seems to be an effective approach, no matter what particular therapeutic approach is taken. For instance, Orlinsky and Howard (1967) report that good psychotherapeutic hours may be collectively described as experiential. They characterize these sessions as being highly symmetrical and collaborative sessions wherein both therapist and client experience a warm, emotionally expressive relationship with each other. Such experiential sessions occur only if the therapist is secure and integrated enough to be able to respond authentically and spontaneously to the evolving situation.

People respond positively and meaningfully to the authentic person. or at least to what they perceive as authenticity. Most people are constantly wary of phonies on all levels, from high government positions to intimate personal contact. The authentic person is perceived as a trustworthy person—even in situations where strong disagreement prevails. While trust is important in daily interactions, it is *essential* in therapy. The client will explore and confront the meaning of personal experience only when there is a belief that the therapist is trustworthy. When therapists take responsibility for and express their anxiety, fear, fatigue, their need to show off, or their need to make a good impression, they will increase the possibilities of the session. Although one cannot guarantee that clients will respond favorably to these disclosures, one can be certain that, unless the therapist owns and expresses personal, meaningful experience, any trust or change is far less likely to occur.

PHENOMENOLOGICAL ORIENTATION

Gestalt therapy (as well as client-centered therapy, psychodrama, existential therapy, and logo therapy) takes a phenomenological stance with regard to the therapeutic relationship. That is, there is a belief that the therapist can work best with the client by entering into the client's phenomenological world, experiencing along with the client the client's perspectives. This orientation requires a close, personal relationship with the client. The therapist cannot be aloof, distant, or totally objective in interaction. The therapist, therefore, needs to be able to understand the client's personal feelings and to respond fully to those feelings.

From the phenomenological perspective, certain therapeutic goals (such as adjustment to the social environment), certain traditional therapeutic techniques (such as exploration of personal history and use of interpretation), and certain methods of focusing on change (such as logical or rational analysis of the situation) are not seen as central in the therapy process and may be counterproductive. Rogers, for example, in *Client-centered Therapy* (1951), emphasizes that the therapist should communicate a sincere, unconditional acceptance of the client and the client's feelings. Perls, too, is directed toward the client's personal experience of the world, and uses this experience as the starting point for further therapy.

The phenomenological perspective also leads the therapist towards concern with the *immediate, current experience* of the client. In fact, in gestalt therapy, it is of paramount importance for the therapist to stay with the client's present experience and to facilitate his or her present awareness. It is through attention to the present, ongoing flow of experience that unresolved personal conflicts emerge and become resolved. This cannot be achieved through a discussion of the past or of noncentral characteristics of the present.

One of the authors had the following experience, which illustrates the difference between exploration of the current experience and of noncentral or past experience. During a graduate training class in gestalt therapy, the instructor assumed the client "role" in order to provide one of the students an opportunity to practice the gestalt therapy technique of *dream work*. In order to do this, the instructor, who did not have a current dream to explore, recalled a dream from the past with the intention of using it to create a practice therapy situation for the student. As the dream work began, the instructor very carefully told the details of the dream to the student, and began what should have been a true exploration of the current personal meaning of the dream. However, the therapist actually began to invent details, to try to recreate old emotional responses to the dream, and to organize the dream so as to provide a good learning experience for the student. This involved much thinking and planning in order to make the experience seem "real." The student, however, quickly realized that the dream was being contrived, and, instead of merely following the program of the instructor, centered his attention on what the instructor actually was doing. That is, he asked the instructor to describe what was really occurring at that moment. With his reorientation away from the dream and toward the current experience of the instructor, the "practice therapy session" became a real therapy session. It led into a meaningful session regarding the instructor's desires to have everything in the environment carefully planned and controlled in advance. Thus, the current experience of planning, organizing, and controlling, once it was explored in therapy, was revealed to be a salient area for personal awareness.

Many times, the client will attempt to fulfill what is assumed to be the expectations of the therapist. When the client tries to alter personal awareness or experience to coincide with the perceived goals of the therapist, the client is playing the role of "good client." That role in itself may be more important for the exploration of current experience than the stated topic. The therapist, therefore, needs to be attuned to the contrived as well as to the spontaneous moments in therapy and to facilitate the honest exploration of true feelings.

ROLES OF THE THERAPIST

Developing the Therapeutic Relationship

A delicate balance between personal and professional responsibilities in the therapy relationship becomes apparent as the therapist integrates personal needs while also developing genuine concern and caring about the person who is seeking growth. By sharing perceptions, feelings, experiences, methods, knowledge, and techniques as they contribute to the clarification of the client's processes, the therapist's behavior itself serves as a model of openness, awareness, and acceptance. At the same time, the therapist is able to recognize a client's polarities, blocks of awareness, defenses, movements away from growth, etc. and is able to apply gestalt therapy techniques appropriately.

Here, we need to clarify one often misunderstood aspect of the therapeutic relationship. When we say "apply gestalt therapy techniques appropriately," do we mean those appropriate for the therapist or for the client? Is the therapist responsible only for self? Does not the therapist have responsibility for the person with whom the therapist works? These questions of technique and responsibility go to the heart of the therapeutic relationship. The answers, to some extent, have to be developed by each individual therapist, but some guidelines can be presented.

In gestalt therapy, it is assumed that maturation involves the ability to generate self-support. A client may come to therapy looking for someone to provide what is not provided from within, but the goal of therapy is to enable the individual to change such dependent, manipulative behavior. The therapist may assume that within each person lies the necessary personal resources for effective and productive living. Certainly, the therapist should not take responsibility for the client's behavior and attitudes nor for the use the client makes of the session with the therapist. Thus, the therapist functions as a catalyst for change without taking all of the responsibility for change within the client. Since people are in charge of their own lives, the therapist can possibly educate them in their own responsibility, but the therapist cannot grow or mature for them. To change and grow is the choice of each client.

Therapists cannot "help" the client in the way that most help is offered. If we attempt to advise or instruct, we will only apply our own answers and awareness to another person's life and experience. Although our answers may be "accurate," "correct," or "beneficial" in that they come out of true perception of some situation, they remain ultimately, *our* answers. Each person has to be able to find answers that are true personally, if the necessary transition from environmental support to self-support is to be made. Ultimately, the therapist is only a resource for the client, a person who may be able to help in the client's discovery of the way to personal awareness.

The gestalt therapist must be aware of any desire to be "a helper," and under what circumstances this desire to "help" surfaces. "Helping" as a means of self-aggrandizement, self-justification, or manipulation is usually destructive in therapy. Even when we have good intentions, the kind of help we have to offer may be suspect. When we affirm each person's uniqueness and ability to generate self-support, we have to discard the notion of having answers for others.

Letting others help themselves affirms the essential value in gestalt therapy—the presence and worth of self-awareness. The therapist who values self-awareness above personal beliefs and values, above cultural and philosophic biases undertakes the experience of being a therapist with "respect and acceptance" for the client, as Gertrude Krause points out (1977). If whatever the therapist does has as its ultimate therapeutic expression the client's uniquely experienced movement toward authenticity, the therapist will find that the matters of concern for each client will reach resolution, the client will approach completeness, and the client will integrate the nonintegrated parts of the personality.

Effective interaction between therapist and client is based upon mutual trust. The client must trust the therapist as a professional who is genuinely interested in working with the client, and the therapist must trust the client to be able to integrate the significance of the therapy into the client's personal framework. In the course of therapy, many times the therapist maintains a relatively noncontrolling stance wherein the client's present awareness is followed more than the therapist's directions. At such times, the therapist functions more as a catalyst for change than as a director of change. We will look at some of the catalyst aspects of the therapeutic relationship in the following pages before turning to more active and directive roles of the therapist.

Applying Therapeutic Techniques

Although it is essential that the therapist provide a tone of open, *honest,* and trusting interaction with a client, such an atmosphere is merely the beginning of the growth possibilities. Once the background for the gestalt experience is established, the therapist is ready to move forward, to clarify the client's needs and wants, to differentiate areas of confusion or emerging polarities, to remove blocks to personal awareness, to express inner experiences fully, and to help the client choose routes toward health. In addition to all of the above, the therapist deliberately frustrates the client by exposing fantasies and beliefs that maintain repetitious, self-defeating behaviors and those that prevent the client from trying new and possibly more satisfying behaviors. Using personal observation and intuition, the therapist assures the client's remaining honest in expressions of present, personal experience, and frustrates the client's use of old and unproductive patterns. In this last respect, any attempts to play the role of a "good client" are frustrated.

Using appropriate means of frustrating the client's usual ways of avoiding growth and change, the therapist often acts as an agent for awareness. That is, the therapist monitors, observes, and points out client responses on levels different from those of the client; for example, by paying attention to body cues, the therapist often becomes aware of ambivalent responses to which the client is not attuned. The therapist may point out that, as the client is saying "yes," body cues are saying "no," or that a particular verbal response seems to be a key to the client's behavior, the significance of that response then may be explored. In short, the position that the therapist holds is informed and perceptive; and, in working with the client, the therapist communicates a valuing of personal awareness. This usually means teaching processes of awareness explicitly (by offering awareness exercises or directed awareness experiments) or implicitly (by being a model of awareness). Educating the client in personal dynamics provides an opportunity for the client to apply what has been learned during therapy to other areas of the client's life.

The client may learn productive ways of interrupting or frustrating unproductive behavioral patterns. As the therapist works with the unproductive behaviors of the client who explores them and discovers the power they are allowed to have, the client begins increased positive self-monitoring. For example, a client of one of the authors worked on his periodic tendency to pull back from people, to withdraw from those with whom he was close. As this tendency was explored, he became aware of his double messages; in certain situations, he would be communicating "I want you and need you," and at the same time "I want to get away from you." This pattern of withdrawing while signaling the need to be close produced confusion and tension between him and his girlfriend. A week after one therapy session in which this pattern had been explored, he reported that awareness of his creating tension had been helpful.

As he explained it, the next time he started to slip into his old pattern of behavior he was sufficiently aware of how he was withdrawing to counteract deliberately his own behavior pattern, to frustrate this tendency. On that occasion, instead of withdrawing, he offered to give his girlfriend a back rub. By moving toward her and by increasing contact instead of diminishing it, he broke the unproductive behavior pattern and opened the expression of his caring and desire to be close.

In order to place at the client's disposal useful and appropriate means of becoming aware of dynamic processes, the therapist calls upon gestalt experiments and techniques that can be introduced effectively. With greater experience and confidence, the therapist can design on-the-spot experiments or modify previous ones situationally. Recently, one of the authors worked with a young man who was trying to decide which of two possible job offers he should accept. He was confused, for, although he could logically and rationally list the benefits and disadvantages for each job, he still was unclear about which one he preferred. Obviously, trying to figure out the solution on a purely rational basis was ineffective. The therapist suggested that he stand with his eyes closed and imagine that he stood at a fork in the road from which paths led to each of the two possible jobs. When he had clearly differentiated their respective characteristics, it was suggested that he allow his body, without deliberation, to move down the path it wanted to travel. There was an almost immediate response. He made definite movement toward one of the choices. His body, as a total organism, knew which path was preferable at that time. This experiment was a useful means of bypassing his intellectualizations about the pros and cons of the choices. Offered to him only as an experiment, it stood as an alternative means of reaching awareness of present desires. After that, it was his own decision to follow the experiment and his decision to accept or reject the results he obtained.

Being open to experimenting and suggesting new ways of approaching an individual's problem means that no set of rules or techniques by themselves will suffice in therapy. There are rules, of course, and there are techniques that the therapist should have available, but the rules are sometimes better ignored and the techniques more effective when generated or adapted on the spot and not blindly followed. Like the experienced and knowledgeable cook who knows the effect of combining ingredients, the experienced and knowledgeable therapist is confident in the novel combinations of experiments devised in sessions with clients. As in the above situation, a therapist may go beyond the superficial techniques when discovering that there are underlying patterns about which one can be cognizant. Clients often have developed complex and rigid systems for maintaining their unhealthy patterns, and they resist change at the same time they ask for it. Change is risky; it may appear to be moving a person into a new, chaotic, and uncontrolled state; it is often quite threatening. The gestalt therapist uses suggestions for experimentation that respect the resistance, support the client's being and choices, and also frustrates expectations, fantasies, or other maneuvers that may take the client away from the experience of threat or fear. The gestalt therapist believes in the ability of all persons to generate within themselves support for effective functioning. The therapist also recognizes that that ability may be buried deeply, and that many persons may choose not to work hard enough or long enough to reach self-support. Perls summarizes the issue in this now classic statement: "To suffer one's death and to be reborn isn't easy" (1969, epigraph).

Seeing Patterns in Therapy

The essence of gestalt therapy is *I* and *Thou, Here* and *Now*. Diagnostic evaluation and history taking are rarely a part of gestalt therapy. Yet, there are patterns to be used when appropriate; that is, there are repeated patterns of behaviors or progressions of psychological states that are lived through by many people. Such scripts or patterns recognized in a therapy situation may be used in meaningful ways to help the client; for example, it is useful to the therapist to understand that people often behave incongruently in situations where they experience some amount of threat to their status, to their relationships with others, or to their self-image, for these are important structures in their lives and they will attempt to maintain them. Thus, it would be a mistake to assume that inconsistency or incongruence in one's client is a conscious attempt to avoid what is happening. Knowing about patterns of incongruence may enable a therapist to highlight the client's willingness to explore personal experience fully.

Observation of incongruence between the client's self-report and the therapist's observations can be a productive point of departure for therapy. The therapist reports personal observations without labeling the behavior as "avoidance" or "resistance" and without interpreting the significance. Likewise, when the therapist recognizes a possible pattern underlying the information received from the client, it can be accepted and integrated into the therapist's repertoire without interrupting the therapy process. Since all the therapist actually can integrate is personal experience and perceptions, the therapist can neither integrate nor interpret events for anyone else. Whatever personal meaning is discovered in therapy comes out of the client's own awareness. The therapist, however, does aid in the differentiating processes that precede affirmation and integration.

If we refer to gestalt learning theory, we see that the "aha" experience, the moment of clear understanding, occurs spontaneously. When the structural relationships of a problem are delineated, when the features are obvious in their functions and as they relate to each other and to the client, the understanding emerges in a solid, well formed, and sharply focused pattern or gestalt. Likewise, in therapy, clarity and sharpness come to the therapist out of awareness of the client's habitual patterns of blocking growth.

The therapist can help differentiate the client's feelings, experiences, and perceptions; however, when that has been accomplished, the client does the rest. For example, the awarenesses of the young man with a career decision were differentiated into imaginary paths through the interventions of the therapist, but the choice and integration of the young man's desires was a spontaneous, individual matter. At the moment of interaction, the client experiences a gestalt completion, an understanding. Experienced therapists report work in which their understanding of a client's experience and the meaning of what was being done was minimal. Yet, by observing the client's obvious behaviors and working only with the sparse information the client has revealed, the therapist facilitates important understandings and discovers that the integrative work of the client has been accomplished.

In using art work as a therapeutic medium, the therapist may have only sparse information and no cognitive understanding of the content being displayed as the client works, yet therapeutic work is being done. One of the authors reports working with a female client who was very blocked in verbal descriptions of an inner image that she sensed was very important. The client was given crayons and newsprint on which she made a series of drawings of the inner image as it changed during the course of an intense, nonverbal fifteen minutes. The client experienced closure, but chose not to share verbally even at that moment. Thus, the therapist had very little information—observation of the drawings and the process of drawing—when the session ended. Many days later, the client reported that she had become aware of the meaning of the drawings she had made.

It is possible, then, for the therapist to proceed through an effective therapeutic encounter and not know details of the client's problem or even know for sure what the problem was. The client may feel closure and not have cognitions related to the therapeutic activity. Such lack of knowledge does not negate the experience, nor does it deny the therapist's value. It reinforces, however, the concept of clients as having the power in themselves to reach understanding without help from someone else. On the other hand, since the therapist is aware of possible patterns, this professional knowledge may suggest avenues that, with skill and knowledge, enable the exploration of dynamics that otherwise are unapproachable by the client.

Let us now consider the topdog/underdog dynamic discussed earlier; much therapeutic activity involves creative ways to deal with this polarity. The names for the two poles of intrapsychic activity may be idiosyncratic to the client, but the psychological configurations of a person's making demands upon the self, and simultaneously sabotaging efforts to meet those demands, fit conceptualizations of intrapsychic conflict as the most powerful conflict a person may experience. The topdog, the part of the person that demands that the person be good, industrious, and moral (similar in some respects to Freud's superego) is aligned against the underdog part, where the person invents excuses for not complying, undercuts efforts, and complains. The dynamic opposition of these two forces may immobilize the individual's resources for growth. If the therapist sees in the client this possible pattern, an exercise that differentiates the two poles and makes their antipathy explicit may be devised.

Once the polarities are clearly differentiated, there is the possibility of resolving the internal conflicts between the two and of freeing energy to be invested in the self, the chooser.

The most relevant and useful patterns to explore in therapy are those, such as topdog/underdog, that block the person from growing and that use energies for dis–ease maintenance rather than for behaviors that are authentic, non-manipulative, and healthy as defined in gestalt terms. Understanding the patterns is important; being able to use them in effective therapeutic interventions is more important. Usually, the more effective uses involve the presentation of observations of presently occurring processes rather than of conclusions about what is or is not happening. Observations may be used to direct the client's awareness toward some undifferentiated behavior. Conclusions are dangerous; the therapist presumes to know more about the client than the client knows. If someone you know, particularly someone you respect and whose opinions are important, tells you that you are avoiding the issue, or that your resistance is showing, that person has drawn a conclusion about your behavior and your motives based only upon that person's experience and perceptions; in dis–ease terms, that person is projecting personal conclusions upon your experience. To state the conclusion permits only responses of acquiescence or rebuttal, both of which turn the encounter into a personal conflict. If you acquiesce in the conclusion, you acknowledge the other person's superiority and may try to change your behavior to fit someone else's opinions. If you argue, you will engage in an encounter in which each participant attempts to justify the disputed perceptions. That kind of encounter between client and therapist is almost always countertherapeutic.

Observations presented as personal experience and for which the therapist takes full responsibility, however, allow the client to see from the therapist's perspective for a moment, to consider whether the observation is applicable or not. Such observations involve the therapist's awareness of unconscious activity that emerges in nonverbal behavior, or of discrepancies between the verbal and nonverbal behaviors of the client. At best, these observations provide an opportunity for awareness. At worst, the client will deviate from the current topic briefly and unproductively, at which time the therapist may suggest other experiments; at best, awareness of another person's observations will synthesize old, immobilizing patterns into an understanding accompanied by clarity and a sense of direction.

Attending to the Obvious

A client's body movements frequently emerge as obviously significant patterns. The therapist may observe, for example, that, as a client reports personal experience, the client's voice quality changes, seating posture shifts, or other bodily movement occurs, apparently without conscious design. Such differences often indicate changes occurring within the client, more obvious to the therapist than to the person involved. When the client's movements become the focus of discussion, the therapist can point out what behaviors are being observed, or ask the client to become aware of what is happening gesturally.

A therapist seldom errs in focusing upon body language. Most people can construct a wall of words, explanations, rationalizations, and justifications around themselves; the language of the body is obvious, clear, and presents concise data for use in therapy. Simkin (1976) points out:

In working with my patients in the "here and now," using the technique of directed awareness—"Where are you now?" or "What are you aware of now?" etc. I have discovered that usually verbal communication is indeed misleading or misdirecting and that body language is not. Thus both the patient and I take his symptoms seriously in that these symptoms—I call them truth buttons or truth signals—communicate how a patient really feels. Thus, if he is in conflict, experimenting with first taking one side of the conflict in fantasy and then the other, he will inevitably bring on the body language, the truth signals, when he takes sides with that aspect of the conflict which is anti-self. (P. 228)

What the client is saying organismically in any situation may be different from what the client *thinks* is being said. The client's self-report may be inaccurate, consciously or unconsciously, and the therapist who is attending to the total communication will hear—aurally or visually—a message that the client is unaware of sending. Therefore, attention to the obvious messages is a prime tool of the therapist. Even though, at times, what is obvious to the therapist may be inaccurate "fantasy" or emotional reactions emerging from the therapist's own confusion about what is occurring, it is better to voice responses than to quell them. Since the therapist is able to share those moments during therapy, it is possible to use personal observations as a means of establishing contact with the client. If the therapist keeps communication open by reporting personal observations and reactions, the client has the opportunity to experiment with the observations conceptually and to determine if they are appropriate or not.

MORE ACTIVE ROLES OF THE THERAPIST

While it has been pointed out that the therapist functions primarily as a catalyst for personal growth in therapy by attending to patterns of avoidance and by responding to the client's body language, the therapist has not been portrayed as an active agent in the client's change process. There are several areas in which the therapist takes more active roles in gestalt therapy; in particular, the therapist takes the most active roles in directed awareness experiments, in finishing unfinished business, and in breaking through the impasse experienced by the client. We will consider each of these roles in the following sections.

Experimenting

Since awareness is considered to be the summum bonum of gestalt therapy, the therapist often is in a position to provide the necessary experiential focus for the client who is seeking appropriate routes to growth. Such focusing typically entails methods or techniques of exposing dynamics that occur beneath the client's present level of awareness. This experimenting stage of therapy can be very productive, both in the one-to-one relationship and in the group relationship. It is the exciting stage of discovery about what people are aware of, what to do to clarify inner processes, and how fast to proceed.

The therapist takes the lead in the experimenting stage by setting up directed awareness experiments, verbal exercises, fantasy trips, body awareness exercises, or interpersonal situations. There may be a particular process that the therapist wants to open for exploration, or there may be concerns of the client that are ready to be explored. Particularly in early group sessions, the therapist may choose to generate large group experiences or dyadic experiences. Yontef (1971) explains how this procedure leads to a different relationship between the therapist and his client or group:

One can question whether the therapist by not attending to his inner response and by concentrating on setting up experiments for the ''Patient'' is not at odds with the I-Thou model or relationship. The Gestalt therapy position is that the therapist makes direct contact with the patient with his senses, attending to an agreed on task, expanding the awareness of the patient. (P. 17)

In one-to-one therapy, an alternative to trying out structured awareness experiments is merely to begin with suggesting that the client report personal experience from moment to moment, no matter how trivial or confused it may seem to be. This simple technique by itself may be sufficient to lead to the heart of the client's problem. The following experience is an illustration of the way in which awareness experiments can affect clarity.

In a clinical psychology training session in which one of the authors was the therapist, a young woman reported that she was trying to decide if she wanted to work on some problems she was experiencing. She had a large range of possible things to work on and was confused. The therapist asked her to relax with her confusion and see what emerged. After a period of quietness she reported that she wanted to do something, but that she still did not know what she wanted to do. Again, the therapist asked her to remain with the confusion, not making a decision but merely letting something surface in her awareness. In a few moments she was detailing a series of professional and personal conflicts that disturbed her greatly. None of them seemed to be more important than the others, and her descriptions flowed from one to the other freely. She had obviously thought a lot and talked a lot about the specific problems. Rather than select one of them, or ask her to select one, the therapist suggested that she consider her list of problems as a whole. Initially, she was surprised at the suggestion. However, as she began to consider the suggestion, she saw how she was confusing herself by trying to concentrate upon a series of complaints or "problems" in rapid succession, rather than concentrating upon the larger gestalt. She also clarified some salient and changeable aspects of the specific situations which troubled her. In this case, what was obvious to the therapist—that there was a common theme in her complaints—was not apparent at all to her. The therapist suggested that the client make a statement regarding the obvious similarities found in all of her complaints. When making such a statement in her own words, the client immediately saw what had been obvious to the therapist for some time. By expressing what was obvious, or "foreground," the therapist added information to the situation, and, in effect, helped her to reorganize her perceptual field.

The hallmark of effective directed awareness exercises, whether they are invented at the moment or are part of the therapist's existing fund of techniques, is their clarifying and unifying functions. Just as the therapist may recognize a larger pattern in the client's behavior the awareness exercises make it possible for the client to attend to the larger patterns also. The expertise of the therapist is necessary, however, in order to know what kinds of exercises are appropriate to the situation.

Facilitating Gestalt Completion

Many problems a client faces fall in the category of "unfinished business." The most significant and important unfinished situation will call out for immediate attention. This tendency on the part of the organism to move toward completion will be mediated by the present experience of what is important to work on, and the willingness to approach what emerges. In therapy, instead of spending much attention and energy in maintaining or futilely trying to complete incomplete situations, the client can be directed toward an awareness of personal responsibility in the blocking of completion of unfinished business. For example, if a client complains of fatigue, chronic restlessness, or a feeling of helplessness without having a specific idea of how these feelings are being produced, the therapist might suggest that the client "stay with" the feeling of fatigue, give it a voice, or give it a physical identity. If the client verbalizes or pictures the experience of fatigue in meaningful ways, closure regarding the internal and external factors that relate to the fatigue can be reached. Often, it is enough to provide momentary clarity for the client to be able to proceed toward resolution; the therapist may not need to intervene directly.

The therapist may also facilitate the bringing to conscious awareness of unconscious unfinished situations in the client by using gestalt exercises as springboards to more concentrated work. For example, a potent group exercise, as designed and reported by Enright (1976), involves simple projection on the part of each member. The therapist may have a box of children's toys and games which is dumped on the floor in the middle of a group. Each person

6 7 5 4 1

is instructed to find one piece which looks most interesting or absorbing. After allowing enough time for the selection process, the therapist then suggests that each person report to the group what the experience of being that toy is like. The experience of projecting oneself into an object and detailing experiences from that perspective often brings out feelings that are associated with unfinished episodes.

Body language, the physical cues perceived by the therapist, may indicate movement toward completing situations. Even when the person maintains control over thinking and does not allow into conciousness the need to reach closure, the body will still be seeking that resolution. On several occasions, we have witnessed a client begin a session with merely a physical experiential description of bodily sensations and then gradually move toward discovering personal responsibility for a headache or a backache or an upset stomach. The physical symptom may be a real, continuing, coping response that the client is unwilling to surrender because it has served so well. There are also occasions when the situation that prompted the response has, in fact, ended, but the mechanism persists almost automatically. This persistent behavior then becomes the target, and the therapist directs the client to become aware of what is being done physiologically. The residual coping mechanism needs to be brought to awareness so the client can then choose whether or not to discontinue it.

Many people, for example, have learned to restrain their words by clenching their jaws; even in situations where they no longer need to be censoring their responses, the clenched jaw remains. Some people exhibit this symptom so strongly that they hardly open their mouths when they speak. Tightened jaws may be inappropriate in present therapeutic situations, but they indicate either that there is much that still needs to be expressed or that this mode of physical response has become habitual. Awareness of the "symptom" of tight jaws can lead to whichever closure is appropriate for the client.

Although learning to control a "symptom" cannot replace actually dealing with the underlying dynamic process and completing the targeted incomplete gestalt, an understanding of the dividing line between dealing with symptoms that persist beyond old situations and symptoms arising from current experiences makes it possible for the therapist to attend appropriately to the experiences of the client. Perls et al. (1951) point out.

. . . throbbing headache, agony of an abscessed tooth, fatigue from overwork, insomnia as an indicator of unfinished business. These are warning signals — they indicate something amiss which needs attention — and the problem is falsely solved when one merely turns off the signal.

With the completion of even a small piece of unfinished business comes a sense of fulfillment for the individual. Present experience is heightened whenever one is able to complete a past experience, for the energy that is tied up in the past then becomes freed and available for the present and future. Although one may have many important unfinished situations, and work on only one of them, the experience of completing gives the client a sense of competence and of ability to complete other situations. As one unfinished situation is resolved, increased energy is released for dealing with other situations.

Working with Resistance

As the therapist works toward closure with the client, honest and seemingly unreasonable resistance may be encountered. The client may not be able to progress beyond a certain degree of differentiation and clarity, yet experience the desire to go farther. The client may become disoriented, confused, hesitant, ambivalent, and may consciously draw the line beyond which the therapeutic encounter may not go.

The essential ingredient in working with resistance in the client is the therapist's willingness to remain in touch with the client's awareness and the choices that are made, while expressing the therapist's personal awareness regarding the continuing therapy experience. Joen Fagan (1970) writing about the task of the therapist is clear in this regard:

Gestalt therapists ask for a clear statement from the patient concerning what he wishes to accomplish. Proceeding from this central theme keeps the emphasis on the patient's stated wishes, not the therapist's expectations. Procedures that keep in the present and make it clear that the therapist is in sensitive awareness with what is happening also decrease resistance. (When a patient begins meeting opposition from his conflicts and the discomfort that surrounds them, he may clearly resist, but this is on a very different order from resistance of control.) The patient is often asked if he would be willing to try an experiment: an acceptance carries a mild commitment to continue while a refusal is honored if a reason is given. The patient who freezes, draws a blank or has nothing come to mind can be asked to verbalize his refusal more specifically or to take responsibility for it by saying, "I am making my mind blank." Another procedure is to go with the resistance ("Tell me that it's no business of mine what you're thinking.") and then have the fantasied therapist answer back. The value of resistance can also be approached ("What are all the good reasons for refusing me now; what does refusing do for you that is valuable for you?"). (Pp. 95-96)

Some people come to therapy, not to change, but to justify their present behaviors or to show their power by frustrating others. When a therapist believes that the client is being manipulative, when there is the feeling of frustration or anger, the therapist can give feedback regarding these feelings, without placing the responsibility on the client. When the therapist is confused, it is best to admit it. The client may have engineered the confusion unconsciously as an avoidance or resistance technique. Clear, honest, and straight forward therapist behavior is essential; the basic trust that evolves in the client/therapist relationship demands that the client see the therapist as a real and authentic person. The therapist's feedback restructures the situation constructively, being expressed descriptively and with responsibility for one's own behavior, instead of making another responsible for it.

Working through an Impasse

If the client is avoiding working beyond a certain point, and if the resistance is not a conscious manipulative behavior, an impasse is reached. Perls defines the impasse as "the crucial point in therapy, the crucial point in growth . . . the position where environmental support or absolute inner support is not forthcoming anymore, and authentic self-support has not yet been achieved" (1969b, pp. 28-29). It is likely that there are catastrophic expectations about what is beyond that point, or there is such a complicated system of avoidance that the client actually cannot know what is expected or what the client is avoiding. Ruth Cohen (1970) states that conceptualization of the impasse situation is the most significant development to come out of gestalt therapy.

The skillful separation of conflicts into their duality and their subsequent reenactment leads, after a series of dialogues, to feelings of blankness, confusion, hopelessness, etc. This experience is the impasse: the ultimate expression of two strivings pulling in opposite directions. The therapist's guiding words are: "be blank," "be confused," "be empty." When the patient can endure and experience the extent of his feelings of confusion, blankness, impotence, etc., organismic change takes place. It is the theory of this impasse phenomenon which I regard as Perls' unique and most important contribution to psychotherapy, both in depth and in speed, in an exhilarating and fruitful way. (P. 137)

The therapist, having worked with the client toward recognition and removal of prior environmental manipulations for support, can help the client discover a route through the point of the impasse by aiding in the generation of organismic support. In general, the therapeutic technique is to concentrate upon the impasse itself. With active resistance, the therapist asks the client to experience the impasse in as complete terms as possible. The therapist needs to maintain two levels of awareness while moving effectively toward breaking through a client's impasse: awareness of the totality of what is occurring moment to moment, and a specific awareness of the details and patterns of the client's responses. Movement through the impasse may be difficult for the therapist if he or she is solely aware of the client's perceptions at that point. That is, if the therapist becomes confused, if the therapist sees only the verbal, or logical, or abstracted conflicts that the client sees, it is difficult to know where to direct attention. At the impasse, the most obvious (and often the simplest) configuration or movement is most serious and important; it is the key to movement through the impasse. Since the client is unaware of the obvious, the therapist has to be aware of it. When the therapist is aware of confusion, that becomes the obvious configuration to be dealt with, and it will lead to the next awareness and the next. When the therapist is able to direct the client to the impasse itself and to how the client blocks progress, the therapist opens the way for exploding out of the situation and into the world of experience beyond.

A dramatic example occurred recently as one of the authors was working with a young woman who, being at a major decision making point in her life, needed to create distance between herself and certain people whom she perceived as making demands upon her. She experimented with ways of telling them that she needed space, yet she was not straightforward verbally and she felt unsuccessful and dissatisfied. After experimenting with several approaches to making clear her underlying demands, the therapist became aware that it was the verbalization itself that held her back from dealing with these people. Her thinking and her words undercut the force and power of her feelings, and she would alter her demands to fit her thinking. At that point, the therapist suggested that she act out her feelings, doing to his outstretched arms what she wanted to do to the people in her life. She proceeded to wrestle furiously with the therapist, transferring her blocked words into actions, and releasing the pent-up energy she had invested in the situation. The impasse was broken through at that moment.

Another way of dealing with an impasse is illustrated in the therapy session transcribed in the appendix. Rather than staying with the moment-by-moment awarenesses of the client, the therapist in this situation chooses to suggest that the client shift attention to a more objective perspective in order to become aware of the internal, conflicting forces that are impacted. A breakthrough is facilitated in this way. These two different processes, both effective in dealing with impasses, again indicate that there is no "right" way to interact therapeutically with a client.

SUMMARY

Through this discussion, we see that, as the gestalt therapist develops in therapeutic work, the awareness that idiosyncratic experiences of clients do not always "go by the book" becomes an internalized reality; that is, many cases do not fit a stated theoretical perspective of gestalt therapy. If the therapist tries to concentrate only upon those dynamics which fit theoretical patterns, he or she may sacrifice the best interests of the client. Therefore, theories alone are not enough; they are modified and mediated by thorough training and by day-to-day experiences in therapeutic encounters. Experience brings a validation of sidetracks, detours, or changes in the context, and it ultimately contributes an ease and sensitivity to the subtleties as well as to the special, momentary whole of any situation. Ease, sensitivity, and creative instincts develop in beginning therapists as they find ways of handling gestalt therapy that best fit their own personalities and styles, keeping in mind always the phenomenological perspective and the radical respect for all of the aspects of every client.

The possibility for deep and powerful therapeutic work that is inherent in the gestalt therapy system, as is illustrated in the transcript in the appendix, demands that therapists be well trained, whether certificated or not; be very clear about themselves, their perceptions, values, their ethical stance, and therapeutic tools; be knowledgeable about gestalt theory and technique; and be able to creatively apply any learnings and spontaneous experimental designs for experimentation appropriately. The system also demands that clients choose therapists with great care.

Responding to the present—its wholeness as well as its constantly emerging figures—is an invaluable ability in any therapist, and even more necessary in gestalt therapy; awareness of the present is one of the basic processes that both the therapist and the client need for intense, powerful, and productive therapy to take place. With the development of present-centered awareness, an I-Thou relationship, a good theoretical road map, and therapeutic tools, the therapist and client move on their separate journeys toward personal growth and fulfillment.

Appendix

Transcript of a Therapy Session

In this appendix we present a transcript of a therapy session, together with comments (in italics), as to the stages in the therapeutic process, the therapist's interventions, and the client's experiences as indicated by his responses, both verbal and nonverbal. The session is presented as it actually happened, with the names of the client and his daughter, and of the places intact, according to the client's wish to help others to understand his experience in the loss of his daughter and in the therapeutic interaction that brought him relief. One of the authors was the therapist in the session.

Step One: Expression

(Therapist takes charge, suggests that client take time to experience rather than report at the overt verbal level.)

(Note: "C" is client; "T" is therapist)

C: What I want to do is set up the situation.

T: (Interrupting) I'd like you to first stop and let yourself settle—take a minute and whenever you feel ready, begin.

C: (Pause of a couple of minutes—deep sigh) About two months ago my daughter died and she's been dying for four or five years and I've not been able to get the feelings going and . . . and know that there is some guilt and some anger but I couldn't handle her telling me that she didn't want to live (begins to cry).

(Therapist supports and encourages expression of feelings.)

T: Yes, just allow your feelings to come . . . .

C: I have a real philosophy that says whatever happens to me I caused and I am . . . deeply believing in spiritual/mind healing. And I wanted to work with her but she didn't believe this, so I knew for me that it was impossible to go to her until she called (holding back tears).

(Therapist again suggests that feelings are okay. It seems that blocked feelings may be the target for the session.)

T: Allow those feelings to come.

C: (Crying) She never called . . . I get so goddamn mad . . . .

(Therapist believes that the scene is set, that the client is experiencing rather than reporting. The client is now ready to experiment. The therapist makes it clear that the client is in charge and has choices about how to proceed.)

T: I'd like to check with you about how you'd like to deal with this.

C: Oh, I haven't the slightest idea, but I do know that there was a lot of ego, connected with the fact that she was number one daughter and was a very attractive thing and just wonderful. To have her check out . . . and, of course, the last memories I had of her were so awful, so absolutely terrible.

Step Two: Differentiation

(Therapist suggests an experimental dialogue.)

T: Do you feel ready to talk to her now, to bring her here in your fantasy?

C: I suppose . . . I, I . . . .

(Therapist keeps client in touch with present experience, encouraging the expression of awarenesses.)

T: Where are you right now?

C: Well, I'm both ways. I'm, I know that I didn't say good-bye to her. I'm really not aware that she's gone, that she's dead. I don't believe that I've accepted that at all. I imagine . . . I expect that I'll go to Santa Barbara and she'll be there.

(Therapist attempts to focus the dialogue keeping the client in charge.)

T: Would you be willing to tell her this? Does that feel right to you?

C: Ah . . . I suppose . . . yes.

(Therapist continues to check client's willingness to proceed and suggests that the client take a major part in structuring the dialogue.)

T: However is more comfortable, with your eyes open or your eyes closed. Take a minute to see her, visualize her . . . when you're ready, begin with whatever you have to communicate to her.

C: (pause) Kathy . . . (T: Yeah) (C begins to cry)

C: I can't believe that you're not here. I'm really sorry that I didn't say good-bye to you—that it didn't seem to be the right time; and when I saw you last you were so . . . so drugged . . . so different . . . so terrible . . . goddamn it, why didn't you . . . (breaks into sobs).

T: Yeah . . . .

C: Why didn't you say something? Why didn't you try to fight it?

(Therapist intensifies the experience.)

T: (repeating client's words) Why didn't you say something? Why didn't you try to fight it?

C: You kept going from remedy to remedy—this was going to do it and that was going to do it, and I got so angry with you. I can't help it. I should have been able to accept you as you were. It's so difficult . . . . (sobs)

T: Yeah.

C: Oh, God, it's difficult (sobbing) . . . it hurts so . . . God almighty!

(Therapist suggests differentiating the feelings and focusing them outward toward the daughter.)

T: Check with yourself and see if you are willing to share some of that hurt, anger, and resentment with her.

C: Yeah . . . you just checked out and left the rest of us here, goddamn it. (sobbing) Life was so good for you. Of course, how would I know for you, but gee, wow, you never had anything tough happen in your life. Life was served up to you on a silver platter with gold around the edges. I resented the fact that you were so damned dependent; you knew that your mother would pay your bills, do anything you wanted, jump through a hoop for you. And all the time she was killing you . . . and that got me angry. If you would have had to face your situation with your income, you'd either have to shit or get off the pot . . . and you refused to see that all of this dependency was bringing the family around that last scene. I was so angry—here you were on the bed, your brother was trying to placate you, the nurse was there offering you melon balls you wanted or some other thing that had to be brought from Hong Kong or around the world—your mother was there—and you were continually wanting more—wanting more—everybody was around. Why, Louis XIV didn't have such an attentive court as you had there—and it got me so fucking angry to see that and to see her.

(Therapist keeps the expression focused and suggests some exaggeration.)

T: Tell her that.

C: Goddamn it, how could you do that? How could you manipulate the whole fucking family? Your brothers were there, not knowing what they were looking at, not realizing they were looking at slow suicide, and you were asking for it, you were asking for every goddamn bit of it!

(Therapist suggests more clarity about the underlying process to encourage overt expression of any remaining feelings.)

T: Check out about her manipulation of you and see if that fits. How is she manipulating you in all of this?

C: Yeah . . . you did it. I made a trip all the way down to Tijuana and you hardly even said "boo" to me. And I just was so hurt inside, and you were the Queen Bee and that nobody else was having any problem, like I wasn't having to move to a new city and a new house. You didn't give a shit about anybody else. It was me . . . me . . . me . . . poor me. You had a goddamn terminal case of poor little me. That really pissed me off . . . a lousy, lousy attitude, Kathy . . . (pause)

(Therapist checks to see if any feelings need to be expressed.)

T: See if there is anything else you want to say to her right now about this—about your anger, feeling manipulated.

(Client begins to discriminate among the feelings.)

C: . . . Well, of course, I did see the other side of it. I could see that your brothers were at least getting in touch with their emotions and . . . but . . . they didn't know what they were seeing, they were supposedly seeing a woman with great courage . . . and you, John, you were in charge of the morphine and codeine and opium and all the rest of the stuff . . . the pills and the injections and the tablets and the whole bunch of stuff . . . (pause)

(Therapist suggests experiment to clarify the polarization of the feelings as the client has experienced them.)

T: Okay. What I'd like you to do if you are willing, is to—now—just allow yourself to let go of these feelings, and I'd like you to shift and become Kathy and let her respond to you.

C: Oh, God . . . Oh, God . . . .

T: Are you willing to do that?

C: I'll try it . . . sheewww . . . .

(Therapist suggests bodily change to help clarify the polarized feelings.)

T: And, if you can, I think it would be really helpful if you shifted positions. Move over there. (Ken changes positions . . . pause) Take a little time to feel what it feels like to be.

C: . . . (begins to sob deeply)

(Therapist lends physical support in the critical point in the experiment.)

T: Yeah . . . (moves physically closer to Ken)

C: It feels like shit . . . Oh God . . . how much hurt.

T: See if you can be there and experience that . . . . What did you call Ken? Dad, or . . . ?

C: Oh, Dad . . . Oh Dad . . . I know you're not interested in the way I feel. I know you're condemning me. I know you didn't believe in my route—I feel as if I'm alone. I like the Mexicans down in Tijuana and I have fun down there. Dr. Carerra is my friend and the other doctors and nurses. I love to talk with them; they are good people. They want to help me. But you . . . sure you came down, and I'm sorry that I wasn't—it was one of my low days and I didn't talk to you—and you were talking a mile a minute to Mary, and you two were having so much fun . . . .

(Therapist slows the work down so that the daughter's statements may be experienced clearly.)

T: Would you tell Dad that again?

C: I'm sorry that I couldn't go your route, Dad. I was on a different route. *I* was on a different route. (chokes on the words)

T: . . . Tell him more about that.

C: I didn't know why I had this feeling of hopelessness. My relationship with Bob hadn't worked out very well. It didn't seem to have any direction; I didn't seem to know what I wanted to do, where I wanted to go, what I wanted to accomplish. And it seemed to me so much more safe to just stay in the nest and let mother pay my bills and be incorporated in her sphere. I did enjoy sort of organizing the International Association of Cancer Victims and Friends, planning their affairs and writing their circulars, but basically I guess I just didn't feel . . . I just felt like I was in a dead end, that there was no real direction, no real reason for me to be . . . . And I guess that was hard for you to understand . . . . (breathes heavily)

Step Three: Affirmation

(Therapist tries to clarify the verbal statement and elicit the feelings associated with the heavy breathing.)

T: What's that?
C: Hard to understand (cries) . . . . God almighty, it was hard to understand.

(Therapist senses that the client has moved away from the role of daughter. He follows the client's process and suggests a role shift.)

T: All right, shift position. Come back and be Ken. I think you have shifted roles.
C: Yeah . . . .

(Therapist slows the work so that the client may experience deeply.)

T: I'd like you just to be still a minute. Close your eyes and just review what she has told you, what she has said . . . and receive that . . . .
C: (begins to cry)

(Therapist suggests the affirmation of the deep feelings.)

T: Just allow that to happen.
C: (crying) I didn't understand! I didn't understand it! It doesn't make any sense at all—no goddamn sense . . . .
T: Yeah, no sense at all . . . .
C: There isn't any sense to that . . . (cries) . . . no sense to that . . . it doesn't make any sense! (blows nose)

(Therapist encourages the client's congruent statement, the central experience.)

T: Can you share that with her?
C: (more composed) I didn't understand that, Kathy.
T: Yeah . . . .
C: I just didn't understand that . . . I'm sorry it just doesn't make any sense.

(Therapist suggests verbal clarification of what the client has said, the completion of the verbal statements.)

T: Can you be more specific with her about . . . how it doesn't make any sense . . . .

(Client begins to clarify both poles of the father/daughter interaction.)

C: Well, yes. You're a beautiful girl with tremendous potential . . . . just the way you related to those Mexicans made me so pleased, and you were so pleased to be able to speak to them in their own idiom. So much conversation—I remember how you told me that you went to a dance with your then current boyfriend who was a Mexican, and you suddenly realized and he suddenly realized that you were the only gringo in the outfit, the only Anglo in the whole room and nobody realized it. And I was so pleased, it seemed like you could make something out of that. And then I remember, too, a clinic in Santa Barbara that was treating the migrant workers, and you had so much fun there 'cause you were able to talk to them and you were able to translate, able to help them. And you didn't denigrate them, you didn't judge them, you didn't treat them as inferiors. You just had some really great things going. I was just excited for you and . . . I don't know . . . I just don't know.

(Therapist asks the client to complete the thought.)

T: What is it that you don't know?

C: I didn't know that that wasn't a calling, a direction . . . why couldn't you make something out of that? Why wasn't that fun? Why wasn't that a reason for living, a reason for moving? A reason—you know damn well that anything that you'd wanted, anything you'd wanted in a way of education or travel or anything—your mother would have given you just like that. (snaps fingers) So it wasn't that you were in some sort of poverty box. You just had no goddamned excuse at all for copping out. What you did, you copped out on us and that's a shitty thing to do. You just gave up, rolled over. That doesn't feel good to me at all.

(Therapist structures the dialogue.)

T: Okay, if it feels right I would like you to shift and be Kathy again and respond to Dad.

C: (sighs and shifts position)

(Therapist takes care that the client experience as deeply as possible so there will be a minimum of unfinished business.)

T: And, again, take just a minute to listen to what Dad has said, how he doesn't understand.

C: (pause) Well, Dad, I did have fun. I did have fun at the intensive language school. And I did have fun relating to . . . Oh, well, you remember when I was working in the kitchen in a Mexican restaurant in Santa Barbara and the Mexicans there were my friends. I did have fun there. And I was able to understand their jokes, and their life, and their feelings. And I didn't know why it wasn't enough. I don't know why my affection for the Tijuana group wasn't enough. You remember when I served down there as a medical assistant without pay and was able to again be a helper in the clinic. I remember how proud I was when I told you that all the clinic felt that I was their baby. You remember when you came down there to surprise me and you asked for me in Spanish, and they didn't know who you wanted, but as soon as you said my name everybody said, oh yes! We know where she is, and that was so pleasing to me. In the middle of that anthill they knew where I was and they knew all about me. All the nurses, all the doctors, I was their baby. And then I got pregnant and then the problem was, would it be possible to have the baby . . . and cancer . . . and everybody down in Tijuana was pulling for me. They really wanted me to have that baby. And I aborted it somehow . . . and I was sad . . . but I guess I just didn't get it together.

(Therapist tries for closure on this part of the interaction.)

T: Is there something more you can tell your Dad to help him understand?

C: (pause) Just . . . I don't know, Dad . . . I guess I just felt that several of these past years I was just marking time, trying to get direction, and somehow it just didn't ever come. And it was so easy to just relax and sleep late in the morning and not have any plan or direction . . . anybody expecting anything from me. I guess I just wanted the easy route. I don't have any explanation . . . . I don't know. My boyfriends were very solicitous. My ex-husband, even a boyfriend of years gone by visited me. And I was pleased to have that concern. Just got that hopeless feeling . . . I know that you sent me a letter telling me that, whereas you accepted my position, that you wanted me to know what your position was without any condemnations, and I guess I was glad to hear that . . . (pause)

(Therapist senses that the dialogue has reached an impasse and suggests a different experiment to facilitate focus and to move the client through.)

T: Okay, Ken, if you're willing I would like to shift a little bit and try something, a different stance. What I would like you to do is to become Ken's objective self—the objective, compassionate, loving observer part of you—and look at Dad and Kathy there and see what you see. Look at what has happened from that perspective. Does that seem right?

C: Yeah, yeah . . . .

(Therapist structures the new material so that the client may be as clear as possible, so that the client may affirm his experience.)

T: You might want to take a different place or stand or whatever feels right to you. (Ken moves to a different place where he can see the two places he has sat in earlier) Take some time to get yourself into that loving, objective place.

(Client begins to affirm the truth of the two positions in the dialogue.)

C: (pause . . . deep breaths . . . .) Well, I see Kathy and I know that she did the best that she could do with what she understood.

T: Um . . . hmmm.

C: She did the best she could. That's hard to say . . . . Oh, that's hard to say (crying) . . . Oh . . . she did the best she could. And I guess Ken did the best he could.

(Therapist anchors the experience in the present so the client may experience congruence.)

T: Imagine yourself looking at Ken, and say that to him.

C: (pause) Yeah, I really think I can say, Ken, that you did what you could. It wasn't very much . . . it wasn't very much. (cries)

(Therapist keeps the roles clear.)

T: Does that feel objective? I'm just checking.

C: Yes, sure it does. (crying) It wasn't very much.

T: I am concerned that you are doing some judging, and I want to make sure that you stay objective.

C: Yeah, it's tough . . . (in deeper voice) . . . and I guess Kathy didn't really feel that you could do anything for her healthwise. *(Client begins to see clear differentiation between father and daughter positions.)* I know, Ken, you felt that you could have opened up the healing power within her . . . had she wanted it . . . and I can see Kathy, who felt that cobalt was a route, but a route that was impossible for her physically . . . and that the chemotherapy, again, was a possible route but it was too terrible for her physically and that she felt that her . . . she actually felt that her vegetarian diet would cure her. And every couple of weeks she had a new diet. And I guess you couldn't quite understand that, Ken. You wouldn't get that . . . so it was tough for both of you to relate in the later stages . . . there wasn't too much to talk about. You really weren't tuned in on the same wave length. *(Client sees clear differentiation.)* I guess I can see that now—on different wave lengths—and all you could do that last day for that two hours that you were with her was to sit there and be absolutely amazed . . . and frustrated . . . and sad . . . all at the same time . . . *(Client affirms personal experience objectively.)* So I guess you, too, did what you could, Ken, with what you knew.

T: Uh-huh.

C: And I guess you were smart not to press yourself or your ideas on her but just to agree that you could to accept her and let her go. But . . . but . . .

(Therapist keeps the differentiation clear, and begins to check for closure.)

T: Just check again and be sure that you are centered and objective, and see if there is anything more you want to communicate to either one of them.

C: . . . Well, I know, Ken, that you were . . . after being with her that last time, you were glad that she went quickly. She was in terrible, terrible pain. And that's why I guess you weren't able to get in touch with a lot of sadness at the funeral. I know that the funeral was a very exciting time for you . . . probably one of the biggest days in your whole life, *(Client continues to affirm personal experience objectively)* but I can see why you weren't able to get in touch with all the sadness and all the frustration at that time. And maybe we are not really able to cope with your not ever seeing her again . . . . (sighs)

(Therapist suggests process for completion of the differentiation process.)

T: Whenever you feel ready, I'd like you to shift back to being Ken, Dad, in your original place. And again take some time to receive.

C: (Pause) Yeah, it was hard to—it *is* hard, in the present, to believe I won't see her again. (pause)

(Therapist checks into immediate experience.)

T: What's going on inside of you right now?

C: Oh, I'm just thinking about that . . . it's (crying softly) . . . it doesn't seem possible. It still doesn't make any sense (sobbing). *(Client makes clear, congruent statement.)* It still doesn't make any sense.

T: Yeah.

C: I don't know if it ever will . . . .

Step Four: Choices and Integration

(Therapist suggests an experiment to discover unfinished business in the dialogue.)

T: Just an idea. I wonder if you would go back to Kathy and say something like, "Kathy, I still haven't accepted that you're dead," or whatever seems right to you.

(Client is resistant to the suggestion.)

C: You mean to be her?

T: No, to talk to her and tell her that you haven't accepted that she's gone.

C: (sigh) (pause . . . crying) Kathy, honey, you just can't believe how tough it is to believe that you're not coming back. Oh, (sobs) that's impossible.

(Therapist suggests statement that may fit.)

T: Yeah, and try out, "and that's what is so hard for me to understand."

C: Yeah, that makes it really tough—really, really tough . . . it is really tough for me to admit that you aren't coming back. That has been a real hard place.

T: Uh-huh.

C: A real hard place. And maybe you can understand that. *(Client brings out unfinished business from the past that contaminates the present experience.)* And, I guess too, Kathy, that you've got to remember that . . . that I think that I have some guilt that when your mother and I divorced that I wasn't able to do for you. Especially when you moved out of town, you moved to Santa Barbara, and oh, I just felt terribly isolated and rejected by the whole group and it wasn't your fault and it wasn't my fault and I guess it wasn't anybody's fault, but . . . so I guess I felt, I felt guilty that there were some things that might have been done that I didn't. *(Client affirms what seems true.)* That probably is an added difficulty here in this situation.

(Therapist suggests a process for closure.)

T: Okay, Ken, time is getting close to the end. What I would like you to do is stay in contact with Kathy for right now. And I'd like you to say goodbye to her in some way, realizing that you can come back to her in fantasy again, or tell her that you will come back—whatever feels right. Say goodbye to her for now, and maybe tell her something of what you still have to deal with in relation to her and what you have done in this session.

C: (pause) Well, Kathy, I do want to . . . whew . . . I do want to say goodbye to you and I want you to know that it's . . . it's been very difficult for me to do this. And that I'm glad we've been able to talk and maybe each of us understands a little more about the situation.

T: Can you share with her what you understand now?

(Client expresses clarity and personal truth at the moment.)

C: Yeah. (in softer, deeper voice) I understand now a little more that you were doing what you had to do. You did the best that you could and I guess you don't really hold anything against me. And I guess you felt that I was doing as good as I could do . . . .

(Client's statements indicate that he is not ready to say goodbye. Therapist suggests recognition and affirmation of the work that still needs to be done.)

T: I'd like you to just consider for a moment what you can now do for yourself based on this, and share that with her—how you can ground this work and make this easier for yourself, accept this more . . . how you can do that, and perhaps what you still need to do.

C: Well, I am pleased that I'm able to do as much as I have done, the changing that I'm doing now and that I have done in the last year. And I know that I did a lot better because of the changes that I've made. *(Client is clear that he has not yet allowed his daughter to die.)* And with you, Kathy, I intend to keep working for more openness and . . . so that I can see a little better where you were coming from. *(Client indicates that some integration may be taking place.)* And accept that you didn't hold anything against me. I like that. I like that a lot. . . .

T: Okay, take a minute and see if there is anything else that you want to do before we stop.

(Client indicates closure for this session with more work to do later. He experiences unblocked energy as relief.)

C: (pause) No, I think that's all I can do . . . (sigh) . . . I feel quite a lot of relief. . . .

End of Session

SUMMARY STATEMENT

This session demonstrates quite clearly the steps in the gestalt therapeutic process as they were discussed in chapter 5. Most of the session is taken up with the steps of expression and differentiation. Near the end, however, Ken affirms himself and his daughter, and he chooses to see each of them as doing the best they could. At this point, some integration of his past polarizations takes place.

After enough expression had taken place to determine where the work would focus, the techniques of dialogue and role reversal were used. These techniques allowed Ken to express and to see his daughter's point of view. He was able to release and express blocked feelings, and considerable clarity was achieved. Ken did not accept or agree with his daughter's perspective, but he was achieving clarity about it. At this point, an impasse developed: Ken was not willing to choose to let go of his gestalt of the situation.

As a possible way to get through the impasse, the therapist suggested that Ken shift to identify with the part of himself that was objective and loving. This experiment enabled Ken to disengage himself from the impasse positions, and allowed him to take substantial steps towards accepting Kathy as she was and toward letting go of his resentment.

Near the end of the session, Ken was able to affirm that he and Kathy were both doing the best they could. He was able to integrate an alienated part of himself when he said, " . . . and accept that you didn't hold anything against me. I like that. I like that a lot."

Although Ken's understanding and acceptance of Kathy's death was not complete, the process of closure had begun.

References

CHAPTER 1

Allport, G. *The use of personal documents in psychological science*. New York: Social Sciences Research Council, 1947.

Bandura, A. *Social learning theory*. Englewood Cliffs, N.J.: Prentice-Hall, 1977.

Cannon, W.B. *The wisdom of the body*. New York: W.W. Norton, 1963.

Combs, A.W.; Richards, A.; and Richards, F. *Perceptual psychology*. New York: Harper, 1975.

Doyle, A.C. A study in scarlet. In W.S. Baring-Gould (Ed.), *The annotated Sherlock Holmes*. Vol. 1. New York: Clarkson N. Potter, 1967.

Goldstein, K. *The organism*. New York: American Book Co., 1939.

Hall, C.S. and Lindzey, G. *Theories of personality* (2nd Ed.), New York: Wiley, 1970.

Kohler, W. *The mentality of apes*. New York: Harcourt, Brace and World, 1925.

Korzybski, A. *Science and sanity*. Lakeville, Conn.: Institute of General Semantics, 1933.

Maslow, A. *Motivation and personality*. New York: Harper & Row, 1954.

Maslow, A. *Toward a psychology of being*. Princeton, N.J.: Van Nostrand, 1962.

Maslow, A. *The psychology of science: A reconnaissance*. New York: Harper and Row, 1966.

Moreno, J.L. *Psychodrama*. New York: Beacon House, 1946.

Ovsiankina, M. Die wiederaufnahme von interbrochenen handlungen. *Psychologische Forschung*, 1928, *2*, 302-89.

Perls, F.S. *Ego, hunger, and aggression: The beginning of gestalt therapy*. New York: Random House, 1969a.

Perls, F.S. Gestalt therapy verbatim. Lafayette, Calif.: Real People Press, 1969b.

Perls, F.S. *In and out the garbage pail*. New York: Bantam Books, 1972.

Perls, F.S., Hefferline, R.F., and Goodman, P. *Gestalt therapy: Excitement and growth in the human personality*. New York: Dell, 1951.

Piaget, J. *The origins of intelligence in children*. New York: W.W. Norton, 1952.

Polster, E., and Polster, M. *Gestalt therapy integrated*. New York: Brunner and Mazel, 1973.

Rosenfeld, E. An oral history of gestalt therapy, Part 1: A conversation with Laura Perls. *The Gestalt Journal*, 1978, *1* (1) 8-31.

Skinner, B.F. *Science and human behavior*. New York: The Free Press, 1965.

Smith, E.W.L. (Ed.) *The growing edge of gestalt therapy*. New York: Brunner/Mazel, 1976.

Suzuki, D.T. *The field of Zen*. New York: Harper and Row: 1970.

Wertheimer, M. *Productive thinking* (enlarged ed.). New York: Harper, 1959.

Zeigarnik, B. Uber das behalten von erledigten und unerledigten handlungen. *Psychologische Forschung*, 1927, *9*, 1-85.

CHAPTER 2

Bateson, G. In an interview with Daniel Goleman. *Psychology Today*, 1978, p. 44.

Buber, M. *I and thou.* (2nd ed.) New York: Charles Scribners Sons, 1958.

Burke, K. *Language as symbolic action.* Berkeley and Los Angeles: University of California Press, 1966.

Cassirer, E. *Language and myth.* New York: Dover Publications, 1946.

Cassirer, E. *The philosophy of symbolic forms.* Vol. 1. *Language.* New Haven & London: Yale University Press, 1955.

Confucius. *Analects.* Quoted in Watts, A. *Nature, man, and woman.* New York: Vintage Books, 1970.

Dewey, J. *Individualism old and new.* New York: Capricorn Books, 1929, 1930.

Durkheim, E. *The elementary forms of religious life.* Trans. by J. Swain, 1912. New York: Collier Books, 1961.

Edie, J.M. Introduction. In Thevenaz, P. *What's phenomenology?* Chicago: Quadrangle Books, 1962.

Erikson, E. *Insight and responsibility.* New York: W.W. Norton, 1964.

Fletcher, J. *Situation ethics: The new morality.* Philadelphia: Westminster Press, 1966.

Heidegger, M. *What is philosophy?* New Haven: College & University Press, 1955.

Husserl, E. *The idea of phenomenology.* The Hague: Martinus Nijhoff, 1970.

James, W. *The principles of psychology*, Vol. II. New York: Henry Holt, 1890. New York: Dover Publications, 1950.

Kelly, G. *A theory of personality: The psychology of personal constructs.* New York: W.W. Norton, 1963.

Kierkegaard, S. *Journals*, Nos. 582-583. New York: Oxford University Press, 1938.

Kierkegaard, S. *Either/or.* Princeton: Princeton University Press, 1944.

Korb, M.P. *Changes in perceptual field characteristics of students in gestalt oriented training.* Unpublished doctoral dissertation, University of Florida, 1975.

Korzybski, A. *Science and sanity.* Lakeville, Conn.: Institute of General Semantics, 1933.

Langer, S. *Philosophy in a new key.* Cambridge: Harvard University Press, 1957.

Levitsky, A., and Perls, F. Rules and games of gestalt therapy. In J. Fagan and I.L. Shepherd (Eds.) *Gestalt therapy now.* New York: Harper & Row, 1970, pp. 140-49.

Maslow, A. *Toward a psychology of being.* Princeton, N.J.: Von Nostrand, 1962.

Mead, G.H. *Mind, self, and society.* Chicago and London: University of Chicago Press, 1934, 1962.

Merleau-Ponty, M. *The essential writings of Merleau-Ponty.* New York: Harcourt Brace, 1969.

Morris, C.W. *Paths of life.* Chicago: University of Chicago Press, 1942, 1956.

Naranjo, C. Present-centeredness: Technique, prescription and ideal. In J. Fagan and I.L. Shepherd (Eds.) *Gestalt therapy now.* New York: Harper & Row, 1970, pp. 47-69

Perls, F.S. *Gestalt therapy verbatim.* Lafayette, Calif.: Real People Press, 1969.

Perls, F.S. *In and out the garbage pail.* New York: Bantam Books, 1972.

Perls, F.S. *The gestalt approach & eye witness to therapy.* Palo Alto, Calif.: Science & Behavior Books, 1973.

Simmel, G. *Conflict & the web of group-affiliations.* New York: The Free Press, 1955.

Suzuki, D.T. *The field of Zen.* New York: Harper & Row, 1970.

Tillich, P. *The courage to be.* New Haven and London: Yale University Press, 1952.

Watts, A. *Nature, man, and woman.* New York: Vintage Books, 1970.

Whitehead, A.N. *Modes of thought.* New York: Macmillan Co., 1938.

Wild, J.W. *Existence and the world of freedom.* Englewood Cliffs, N.J.: Prentice-Hall, 1963.

Wild, J.W. *The challenge of existentialism.* Bloomington, Ind.: Indiana University Press, 1966.

Wilhelm, R. Trans., English by C.F. Baynes. *The I Ching or book of changes.* Princeton, N.J.: Princeton University Press, 1950.

Zijderveld, A.C. *The abstract society.* Garden City, N.Y.: Anchor Books, 1970.

CHAPTER 3

Bandler, R., & Grinder, J. *The structure of magic.* Palo Alto, Calif.: Science and Behavior Books, 1975.

Cassirer, E. *Language and myth.* New York: Harper and Brothers, 1946.

Combs, A.W., & Snygg, D. *Individual behavior.* New York: Harper & Row, 1959.

Denner, B. Deception, decision-making, and gestalt therapy. In J. Fagan and I.L. Shepherd (Eds.) *Gestalt therapy now.* New York: Harper & Row, 1970.

Ellis, A. Rational psychotherapy. *Journal of General Psychology,* 1958, *59,* 36-49.

Erikson, E. *Identity: Youth and crisis.* New York: W.W. Norton, 1968.

Frankl, V. *Man's search for meaning.* New York: Washington Square Press, 1959, 1963.

Goldstein, K. *The organism.* New York: American Book Co., 1939.

Horney, K. *Our inner conflicts.* New York: W.W. Norton, 1945.

Kelley, E. The fully functioning self. In *Perceiving, behaving, becoming: A new focus for education.* Washington, D.C.: Association for Supervision and Curriculum Development, 1962, Pp. 9-20.

Kelly, G.A. *A theory of personality: The psychology of personal constructs.* New York: W.W. Norton, 1963.

Korb, M. P. The function of language in identity formation. Unpublished manuscript, 1974.

Lacan, J. *The language of the self: The function of language in psychoanalysis.* New York: Delta, 1975 (originally published in Paris, 1956).

Langer, S. *Philosophy in a new key.* New York: New American Library, 1951.

Lewin, K. *Field theory in social science: Selected theoretical papers.* New York: Harper & Row, 1951.

Maslow, A. *Motivation and personality.* New York: Harper & Row, 1954.

Maslow, A. *Toward a psychology of being.* Princeton, N.J.: Van Nostrand, 1962.

Maslow, A. *The farther reaches of human nature.* New York: Viking Press, 1971.

May, R. *Love and will.* New York: W.W. Norton, 1969.

Mucchielle, R. *Introduction to structural psychology.* New York: Funk and Wagnalls, 1970.

Perls, F. *Ego, hunger, and aggression: The beginning of gestalt therapy.* New York: Random House, 1969a.

Perls, F. *Gestalt therapy verbatim.* Lafayette, Calif.: Real People Press, 1969b.

Perls, F. *In and out the garbage pail.* New York: Bantam Books, 1972.

Perls, F., Hefferline, R.F.; and Goodman, P. *Gestalt therapy*. New York: Dell, 1951.
Rogers, C.R. *Client-centered therapy: Its current practice, implications, and theory*. Boston: Houghton Mifflin, 1951.

CHAPTER 4

Berger, P.L.; Berger, G.; and Kellner, H. *The homeless mind: Modernization and consciousness*. New York: Random House, 1973.
Bugental, J.F.T. *The search for authenticity*. New York: Holt, Rinehart and Winston, 1965.
Gendlin, E. *Experiencing and the creation of meaning*. New York: Free Press, 1962.
Lowen, A. *The betrayal of the body*. London: Collier Macmillan, 1967.
Maslow, A. *Motivation and personality*. New York: Harper & Row, 1954.
Maslow, A. *Toward a psychology of being*. Princeton, N.J.: Van Nostrand, 1962.
Naranjo, C. Present-centeredness: Technique, prescription and ideal. In J. Fagan and I.L. Shepherd (Eds.) *Gestalt therapy now*. New York: Harper & Row, 1970. Pp. 47-69.
Perls, F.S. *Gestalt therapy verbatim*. Lafayette, Calif.: Real People Press, 1969.
Perls, F. *In and out the garbage pail*. New York: Bantam Books, 1972.
Perls, F. *The gestalt approach & eye witness to therapy*. Palo Alto, Calif.: Science and Behavior Books, Bantam Books edition, 1973.
Perls, F.S.; Hefferline, R.F.; and Goodman, P. *Gestalt therapy*. New York: Dell, 1951.
Reich, W. *Character-analysis*. New York: The Noonday Press, a division of Farrar, Straus & Giroux, 1949.
Rogers, C.R. *Client-centered therapy: Its current practice, implications, and theory*. Boston: Houghton Mifflin, 1951.
Rolf, I.P. What is rolfing about? *Bulletin of Structural Integration*, 1977, 6 (2), 1-7.

CHAPTER 5

Bandler, R., & Grinder, J. *The structure of magic*. Palo Alto, Calif.: Science and Behavior Books, 1975.
Beisser, A. The paradoxical theory of change. In J. Fagan and I.L. Shepherd (Eds.) *Gestalt therapy now*. New York: Harper & Row, 1970.
Edie, J.M. Introduction. In M. Merleau-Ponty, *The primacy of perception*. Evanston, Ill.: Northwestern University Press, 1964. Pp. xiii-xix.
Gendlin, E. *Experiencing and the creation of meaning*. New York: Free Press, 1962.
Gendlin, E. Values and the process of experiencing. In A.R. Mahrer, (Ed.) *The goals of psychotherapy*. New York: Appleton-Century-Crofts, 1967. Pp. 180-205.
Greenwald, J.A. The ground rules in gestalt therapy. *Journal of Contemporary Psychotherapy*, 1972, 5, (1) 3-120. Reprinted in C. Hatcher and P. Himelstein (Eds.) *The handbook of gestalt therapy*. New York: Jason Aronson, 1976. Pp. 267-80.

Hatcher, C., and Himelstein, P. (Eds.) *The handbook of gestalt therapy.* New York: Jason Aronson, 1976.

Korb, M.P. *Changes in perceptual field characteristics of students in gestalt-oriented training.* Unpublished doctoral dissertation, University of Florida, 1975.

Korb, M.P., and Themis, S. The importance of group process in gestalt therapy. *Journal for Specialists in Group Work,* 1980, 5, 1. Pp. 36-41.

Krause, G. *Some notes on gestalt therapy training.* Monograph, privately printed, 1977.

Leviksky, A., and Perls, F.S. The rules and games of gestalt therapy. In J. Fagan and I.L. Shepherd (Eds.) *Gestalt therapy now.* New York: Harper & Row, 1970.

Merleau-Ponty, M. *The primacy of perception.* Evanston, Ill.: Northwestern University Press, 1964.

Naranjo, C. Expressive techniques. In C. Hatcher and P. Himelstein (Eds.) *The handbook of gestalt therapy.* New York: Jason Aronson, 1976. Pp. 281-305.

Perls, F.S. *Gestalt therapy verbatim.* Lafayette, Calif.: Real People Press, 1969.

Perls, F. *The gestalt approach & eye witness to therapy.* Palo Alto, Calif.: Science and Behavior Books, Bantam Books edition, 1973.

Perls, L. In E. Rosenfeld, An oral history of gestalt therapy, Part 1: A conversation with Laura Perls. In *The Gestalt Journal,* 1978 1 (1), 8-31.

Pfeiffer, J.W., and Pfeiffer, J.A., A gestalt primer. In *The 1975 Annual Handbook for Group Facilitators,* La Jolla, Calif.: University Associates Publishers, 1975. Pp. 1-9.

Polster, E., and Polster, M. *Gestalt therapy integrated.* New York: Brunner and Mazel, 1973.

Rogers, C.R. A theory of therapy, personality, and interpersonal relationships, as developed in the client-centered framework. In S. Koch (Ed.), *Psychology: A study of a science. 3. Formulations of the person and the social context.* New York: McGraw-Hill, 1959. Pp. 184-256.

Yontef, G. *A review of the practice of gestalt therapy.* Privately published, available from The Trident Shop, California State University, Los Angeles, California, 1971.

Zinker, J. *Creative process in gestalt therapy.* New York: Brunner/Mazel, 1977.

CHAPTER 6

Cohen, R.C. Therapy in groups: Psychoanalytic, experiential, and gestalt. In J. Fagan and I.L. Shepherd (Eds.), *Gestalt therapy now.* Palo Alto, Calif.: Science and Behavior Books, 1970. Pp. 130-39.

Enright, J.B. Thou art that: Projection and play in therapy and growth. In C. Hatcher and P. Himelstein (Eds.), *The Handbook of Gestalt Therapy.* New York: Jason Aronson, 1976. Pp. 469-76.

Fagan, J. The tasks of the therapist. In J. Fagan and I.L. Shepherd (Eds.) *Gestalt therapy now,* Palo Alto, Calif.: Science and Behavior Books, 1970. Pp. 88-106.

Fiedler, F.E. A comparison of therapeutic relationships in psychoanalytic , nondirective, and Adlerian therapy. *Journal of Consulting Psychology,* 1950, *14,* 435-36.

Krause, G. *Some notes on gestalt therapy training*. Monograph, privately printed, 1977.

Orlinsky, D.E., and Howard, K.I. The good therapy hour: Experiential correlates of patients' and therapists' evaluations of therapy sessions. *Archives of General Psychiatry,* 1967, *16,* 621-32.

Perls, F.S. *Gestalt therapy verbatim*. Lafayette, Calif.: Real People Press, 1969.

Perls, F.S.; Hefferline, R.F.; and Goodman, P. *Gestalt therapy*. New York: Dell, 1951.

Rogers, C.R. *Client-centered therapy: Its current practice, implications, and theory*. Boston: Houghton-Mifflin, 1951.

Simkin, J.S. The development of gestalt therapy. In C. Hatcher and P. Himelstein (Eds.) *The handbook of gestalt therapy*. New York: Jason Aronson, 1976. Pp. 223-33.

Yontef, G.M. *A Review of the practice of gestalt therapy*. 1971. Privately published, available from The Trident Shop, California State University, Los Angeles.

Name Index

Subject Index

Acceptance. *See* Affirmation

"Acting" in therapy, 14-15, 74-75, 83, 90-91

Affirmation. *See* Steps in therapeutic process

Aggression, 22-23, 38, 40-41, 66-67

Alienation/identification. *See* Personality dynamics

Anxiety, 56-57, 60-61, 69, 76, 85

Approaches to therapy, related to gestalt therapy
  behavioral, 15-17
  humanistic, 13, 89
  neoanalytic, 14-15
  psychoanalytic, 10, 13-14
  psychodrama, 14-15
  rational-emotive, 42-43
  Reichian, 15

Art as therapeutic tool, 96

Assimilation, 37-38, 39-40, 41-42, 48-49, 57, 60

Authenticity. *See* Health
  in therapist. *See* Therapist

Avoidance, 16, 17, 95, 98

Awareness, 15, 16, 17, 18, 22-23, 24, 26-27, 28, 29, 30, 32-33, 34, 38, 40-41, 46-47, 48-49, 56, 59-60, 64, 67, 76-77, 78-79, 80-81, 92, 93, 94, 102

Axiology, 20, 29-34

B-cognition (Maslow), 40-41, 67

Behaviorism. *See* Approaches, Behavioral

Body, aspects of in therapy
  armor, 15
  as symbol or sign, 25-26, 62
  language, 33, 97-98, 100-101
  sensing experience in, 15, 26-27, 41-42, 48, 49-50, 65
  use of, in therapy, 76-77, 97-98, 100-101, 104

Catastrophic expectations. *See* Expectations

Cause-and-effect processes, 7, 26-27

Change, 16, 70-71, 73-75, 85
  prevention of, 71-73

Choice, 7, 16, 17, 18, 24, 27-28, 29, 30, 31, 33-34, 39, 58, 59-60, 70-71, 78-79, 80-81

Closure of gestalten, 37, 52, 61-62, 81, 83-84, 95, 99-102

Cognition, 42-43, 44, 96

Conflict, intrapsychic, 76-77

Confluence. *See* Denial of personal experience

Congruence, 45, 59-60, 81

Contact function of self/ego, 22-23, 36, 38, 42-43, 45, 47-49, 51, 59-60, 67, 83, 84-85

Contact/withdrawal. *See* Personality dynamics

Control, 37-38, 45, 46-47, 59-60, 61-62, 66-67

Coping styles and mechanisms, 16, 60, 64, 70-71

"Creative precommitment," 12

Defense mechanisms, 13, 56, 62, 64

Demands, 51-52

Denial of personal experience, 64-68
  projection, 15, 64-65, 83, 100-101
  introjection, 31, 63, 66
  retroflection, 50-51, 66-67
  confluence, 66-68

Dependency, 50-51, 62-64

Depression, 56-57

Dialogue. *See* Techniques

Differentiation. *See* Steps in therapeutic process

Directed awareness experiments. *See* Techniques

Dis-ease, 59-68
  definition of, 39-40, 47, 53-54
  denial of personal experience. *See* Denial
  expressions of, in anxiety. *See* Anxiety
  leaving gestalten incomplete, 37-38,

125

About the Authors

Vernon Van De Riet received his graduate training in clinical psychology at Florida State University, and completed his internship at the Judge Baker Guidance Center and Harvard University Medical Center in Boston. For the past seventeen years he has been on the faculty of the Department of Clinical Psychology at the University of Florida. Dr. Van De Riet is a pioneer of gestalt therapy training in university settings. Since 1969, he has experimented with a variety of ways to train students in the gestalt approach. He is also interested in integrating gestalt methods of with other forms of psychotherapy. Currently, (1979-80) he is on leave of absence from the University of Florida and is training and practicing in Pasadena, California.

Margaret P. Korb, called Pat by her friends, is an instructor at Santa Fe Community College and co-director of the Gestalt Center in Gainesville, Florida. At the college, she has been involved for several years in human services training, particularly in the development of competencies and external degree structures. She has been a therapist and trainer in gestalt therapy for eight years in graduate level courses and in private practice through the Gestalt Center of Gainesville. She has an M.A. in English and a Ph.D. in Counselor Education from the University of Florida. Receiving the doctorate in 1975 fulfilled a promise made to herself when she received her B.A. in 1939. She is particularly interested in the spiritual and healing aspects of therapeutic work. She is a certified clinical mental health counselor, listed in the Register of the National Academy of Certified Clinical Mental Health Counselors, 1979-1980. Recently she became an associate member of the Gestalt Therapy Institute of Florida.

John Jeffrey Gorrell is an assistant professor in the Education Department at Southeastern Louisiana University where he teaches educational and developmental psychology and counseling. Dr. Gorrell's academic interests include phenomenological and cognitive components of learning, as well as psycholinguistics, counseling, and stress management. His research and writings span such areas as general semantics, gestalt therapy, bilingualism, teacher stress and anxiety, and social development. In the past few years he has co-led gestalt therapy groups, been director of training for Tangipahoa Crisis Phone, and engaged in personal counseling. Dr. Gorrell received his Ph.D. in Educational Psychology from the University of Florida in 1975.